NOT
EASILY
SHAKEN

NOT EASILY SHAKEN

Overcoming Personal Challenges in the Face of Adversity

BERT MULLINGS

ARCHWAY
PUBLISHING

Archway Publishing books may be ordered through booksellers or by contacting:

Archway Publishing
1663 Liberty Drive
Bloomington, IN 47403
www.archwaypublishing.com
1-(888)-242-5904

Scripture taken from the New King James Version®. Copyright © 1982
by Thomas Nelson, Inc. Used by permission. All rights reserved.

We want to hear from you. For speaking engagements, books and other resource
information contact the author at: bertmullings@gmail.com; or write to us at:

Bert Mullings
P.O. Box CR-54027
Nassau, The Bahamas

Or visit www.Archway Publishing.com/bookstore

ISBN: 978-1-4808-0407-4 (sc)
ISBN: 978-1-4808-0408-1 (e)

Library of Congress Control Number: 2013955392

Printed in the United States of America

Archway Publishing rev. date: 2/10/2014

CONTENTS

DEDICATION

This book is dedicated to my wife and lifelong friend who has been a strong support system and a tower of strength during my valley experiences. To my daughter, Frecinda, and sons, Prince and Bershawn, thank you for your prayers, strength and unity. To my new twin brother, Wellington, who has given unselfishly of his time, resources, and stem cells to assist in my recovery and divine healing, thank you.

To Randy and Rona Butler, dear friends, thank you for investing seeds of empowerment into my life; and thank you to Nathaniel Adderley, Theresa Deleveaux and the team for making things happen for me. To my wife's Cable Bahamas family, my sincere thanks. To my eight brothers and four sisters thank you for your support.

To the millions of individuals who are suffering from a disease, as well as those who have been given a death sentence report by their doctors, I encourage you to read this book, embrace the process, decree and declare the Word of God, and then speak into the atmosphere and believe in the Great Physician, The Healer and Giver of life, to heal you.

To Jesus, my Big Brother, the Spoken Word of my Heavenly Father that sends His Word to us during our valley experiences and provides us with the manna, strength and encouragement we need to overcome and walk in victory of our healing, my heartfelt thanks.

To the Holy Spirit, my Mentor and Life Coach, who executed The Word in my life, powering me behind the veil and illuminating His presence during my valley experiences, my sincere thanks.

FOREWORD

NOT EASILY SHAKEN is an erudite, eloquent, and immensely thought-provoking work that gets to the heart of the deepest and most common human experience of facing and effectively dealing with life's unexpected twists and turns. We will all face some form of trauma or challenge that will test our faith and cause us to question providence.

This is indispensable reading for anyone who wants to learn how to live in the face of tragedy and trauma and to respond effectively while rising above the storms of life. This is a profound authoritative work, written from the valley of experience from the heart of a man who has been there, that breaks new ground in its approach and will possibly become a classic in this and the next generation.

This exceptional work by Bert Mullings is one of the most profound, practical, principle-centered approaches to this subject of persevering in the face of trials that I have read in a long time. The author's approach to this timely issue for many in these troubled times brings a fresh breath of air that captivates the heart, engages the mind and inspires the spirit of the reader to believe in the impossible.

The author's ability to leap over complicated theological and metaphysical jargon and reduce complex theories of life to biblically sound yet simple and practical principles that the least among us can understand is amazing.

This work will challenge every human, including the intellectual, while embracing the laymen as it dismantles the mysterious soul search of mankind to deal effectively with the misfortunes and unexpected mountains that rise in their lives. This book delivers the profound in simplicity.

Bert Mullings' experienced-based approach immediately identifies with the human heart and awakens in the reader the untapped inhibiters that retard our personal ability to overcome the odds. The author's use of his personal anecdotes empowers us to rise above these self-defeating, self-limiting factors to a life of exploits in spiritual and mental attitudes that bring us victory no matter the challenge.

The author also integrates into each chapter time-tested biblical precepts, giving each principle a practical application to life that makes the entire process people-friendly.

Every sentence of this book is pregnant with wisdom, inspiration, encouragement, edification and passion and I enjoyed the mind-expanding experience of this exciting work. I admonish you to plunge into this ocean of knowledge and watch your life change for the better as you face your challenges in life and you will also come to believe that you are *Not Easily Shaken*.

Dr. Myles Munroe
BFM International
ITWLA
Nassau, Bahamas

PREFACE

In this world all of us will experience tribulation, tragedy and some level of trauma that seek to rock the very fiber of our being, our faith and our trust in whatever God we pay homage to. The reality is, whatever challenges we face, we are not exempt because of our social, economic and/or political affiliations. Whether we are poor, rich, black or white we will all taste a level of hell and will continuously have to pass various tests to get to the next level in life. In fact, all of us have to endure and bite the bullet of life and find some way, by hook or by crook, to deal with our personal challenges. If we do not address these life-threatening and soul-searching challenges, then life will make an example out of us, and we will reap the consequences of our poor decisions.

Many of us are big talkers, forever claiming that we can do anything and everything so much so that nothing can take us down, or so we think! The truth of the matter is, even a fool realizes that if he holds a big block of ice in his hands long enough, he can freeze to death. If we think we are invincible and nothing can rock our world to the point that drives us almost to the place of insanity, because of the pain and suffering we have to endure, then we are lying to ourselves and the truth is not in us.

I can tell you that I have been to that place. I visited hell and saw a glimpse of death but I refused to sit on the sidelines of life and do nothing. I have learnt through my personal experience that no storm is worth fighting if I am not connected to the One who has the power to control and calm the storms in my life. My strength and power is inadequate. I need God! I need God as my rock and my foundation. I need Him to be my fortress and strong tower when the storms of life hit me like a ton of bricks. When I stand, I stand confident knowing that no matter what life's curve balls are hurled at me, I am not easily shaken.

This book, therefore, seeks to address how best to respond to life's challenges and how to overcome them in the face of adversity. This book takes you on a journey of my personal experience that turned my world upside down, inside out and 180 degrees in a different direction all at one time; as well as how I focused on my response to this challenge. This book also addresses very deep issues that all human potential will face in times of tragedy and trauma— that is, the pity party syndrome and the blame game, and then the age-old question we often ask, "Where is God in all of this?" It also addresses and provides time-tested principles that we can follow so that we are not easily shaken in our walk with God.

It is my prayer that once you have read this book you will experience a transformed mind, a renewed spirit and a sense of urgency to fulfill God's mandate for your life. These time-tested principles will help you to begin the process of preparing and perfecting the art of a not easily shaken lifestyle that only comes from an intimate relationship with the Creator. Whatever storms in life we have to face, remember that we were sent to earth to fulfill a mission. We have the power, through the Holy Spirit, to overcome personal challenges in the face of adversity.

ACKNOWLEDGEMENTS

I thought that one of the greatest tragedies in life is dying and having your potential unfulfilled. Well, based on my latest encounter with God, I had to recalibrate my theological understanding for another tragedy is living our lives unprepared to face the challenges head on that will come. No one is immune from tragedy or trauma; but it comes to test and strengthen our faith because we are destined for a purpose. Additionally, God wants us to empower our lives with His presence.

Many of us pretend that we are so tough because we act like we are made of steel. However, if we hold ice long enough even the strongest of men will shiver and/or freeze to death. I acknowledge God as the Source of my life and He is my **Jehovah Rapha - The Healer**. Without Him in my life guiding and protecting me throughout this experience, I would be a living wreck and may have even given up on life itself. I am confident that He did not leave my soul in hell, and He never left me during my test, even though He was silent most of the time.

I acknowledge that God is in total control and, when the fullness of time comes, He allows us to go to a place called, *"paused for a purpose"*. This place, in my opinion, is like a wake-up call that drives us to a point where we conclude that we not only have a mission to fulfill, but we are also empowered and destined to live for God in spite of our shortcomings and insecurities.

I acknowledge that Jesus Christ is the Son of God and my **"Big Brother,"** who is continually making intercession on my behalf to my Heavenly Father—the Source and Giver of life. I acknowledge the presence of the Holy Spirit, the Governor of Earth, who was sent to reside and execute His Heavenly mandate in my life and keep me pure until the return of the Lord Jesus Christ.

I want to personally thank my wife for her unselfish support and strength during my time of testing and the sacrifices that she made, which will never go unnoticed.

Also, special thanks is extended to our editing consultant, Andrea Miller-Curling, who offered invaluable advice for this work as well as all those who prayed, visited and encouraged me throughout my valley experiences. May God forever bless you all!

Finally, I acknowledge that I was born for a purpose and sent directly from the chambers of Heaven as part of God's Master plan so I have to submit to His authority and Lordship to ensure that I do not miss Him in the process. Even though my earthly passport says I am a citizen of the Commonwealth of The Bahamas, I am not of this world—I am an ambassador of the Kingdom of Heaven. I was sent to influence earth with the message of the Kingdom of God.

Even though the ethnos of the English language considers satan as a pronoun and his name should be capitalized, the author has intentionally violated this principle and limits the name of satan and the devil in lower case.

Even though the ethnos of the English language considers satan as a pronoun and his name should be capitalized, the author has intentionally violated this principle and limits the name of satan and the devil in lower case.

C H A P T E R 1
HOW IT ALL GOT STARTED...

At the age of 11, I decided that I would give my life to Jesus. At that time it was not the most popular thing to do; but I believed in my heart it was the right thing to do. Even though I grew up in a Pentecostal church, it was hard for me to deny that God was real because I always felt His presence in my life. This was what I wanted. I wanted to know God and have a personal relationship with Him. I also understood that the price tag was high and I would have to overcome many challenges and temptations as a young man growing up. **"These things I have spoken unto you, that in me ye might have peace. In the world ye shall have tribulation: but be of good cheer; I have overcome the world." (John 16:33)**.

Then at the age of 15, I spent many evenings and weekends on the streets with my parents who hosted street meetings and, thus, I was exposed to and saw the healing power of God in action. **It was like "awesome"!** These experiences further increased

1

my faith in God and I was totally convinced that I had to sell out to God in a deeper way.

I spent most of my teenage years in church where I was mentored in the Word. I also preached many sermons and realized that God has called me to do a work; however, He remained silent in His calling for a very long time, at least it seemed that way. Rededicating my life to the Lord was something I had to do to prove to God that I was committed to doing whatever He wanted me to do even though I did not know what the mission was.

At age 37, when I least expected it, God showed up in my life. Was I surprised? Oh yes, I was because He showed up in a place that I least expected. It was the place of my birth, the island of Abaco. God spoke to me, and, for the first time, I was assured that God had honored my commitment to living a holy life. **"For I know the thoughts that I think toward you, saith the Lord, thoughts of peace, and not of evil, to give you an expected end" (Jeremiah 29:11).** The theme of our encounter was called, "Kingdom Empowerment".

satan attacks my Economic System

After graduating from Savannah State University with an honors business degree in Marketing in 1994, I returned home to The Bahamas in 1996, where I officially began my marketing career with a public corporation. I started out working with small businesses, assisting them by developing marketing plans, initiating public relations efforts, as well as identifying markets for product distribution. In addition, I also provided technical advice and trained small business persons to enhance their knowledge base in marketing.

After working hard and investing long hours in assisting small business persons, I was eventually promoted to Manager of Marketing and Public Relations. This position provided me with the opportunity to focus on obtaining more contracts for local manufacturers, developing a small business directory as well as promoting my employer as a small business development corporation. I also played a vital role in the development of the corporation's new thrust, "domestic investment".

It became quite apparent that I was envied and hated for the level of success that I had achieved working as a manager as well as "getting what I wanted", as has been quoted to me over and over again. The reality was, the favor of the Lord generated positive results in my workplace. For some of my colleagues, this was not well received. In my opinion, there was a deliberate attempt to terminate my services because in September 2002, after six years of employment with the corporation, I was disengaged.

satan's attack on my economic system initially felt like a blow to my gut. Obviously, I was never fired in my life. I had a wife, three small kids and was renting an apartment. It seemed like the only thing for me to do was to start pressing panic buttons. However, I did not. I was reminded of a quote from the King's Constitution, **"And we know that all things work together for good to them that love God, to them who are the called according to *his* purpose." (Romans 8:28).**

I maintained a positive attitude and was convinced that the Source of my peace had promoted me instead of demoting me. In other words, in the physical realm a termination is considered a demotion; however, **in the spiritual realm, a termination is considered a promotion.** Even though I did not see the physical manifestation of the promotion instantly, I believed it was just a matter of time.

Throughout my entire experience of being unemployed, I sought the Lord and I did find comfort. **I decided not to roll over and allow the pressures of life to make a victim out of me** because I realized who was behind the attack on my economic system. **If satan attacks our economic system and we allow him to get away with it, then we will become his prostitutes.** The same thing that satan was fighting me on, **I did not run from it; I ran toward it!**

The attack on my economic system was a violation of my right to provide for my family as well as have more than enough to honor God with. I was not going down without a fight, however—that is, a fight to keep everything that God had already blessed me with. Can you imagine someone coming into our home to stay with us and then dictate to us what we would eat, how many hours we would have to work, tell us when we could take a break and finally, take control of our finances without our permission? This is what the devil was trying to do. He was trying to rage financial havoc on my economic system.

What did I do that was so life changing? My initial response was, that devil is a crossed-eyed liar! I started a consulting company and hit the pavement running to provide for my family. The conclusion of this season of attack on my economic system resulted in me not losing any of the assets that I had acquired before I was disengaged. It also paved the way for me to complete my first customer service book called, "Principles of Customer Service—A Systematic Approach to Customer Service Delivery". This book was published in 2008.

satan attacks my Family System

Many of us are of the opinion that once we serve God and have a family that we are exempt and/or immune from an attack of the enemy on our family system. It was the family structure and its systems of operation that satan attacked in the beginning in an effort to destroy one of the most powerful institutions on earth—the family structure. satan realizes that if he can get into the family structure through any means possible, it gives him the opportunity to plant seeds of sin and iniquity. He is also intentional in his planning and strategy to the point that he wants to create havoc and sustain his presence in the lives of human beings from one generation to another.

However, it is up to us as men to take charge of our families and lead the way to guard against satan winning the battle of tearing families apart. It is also up to us as men to not only position ourselves as priests in our homes, but also as leaders of our communities. We need to build strong ties with our sons and daughters, imparting the Word of God in their lives so that they can stand against the wiles of the devil. So the question is not whether the devil will attack the family structure, but when will he attack it! Therefore, it is imperative to be prepared when he plans his assault. He attacks the family structure in the following ways: He

- steals the joy of the family through fear, tragedy, sickness and disease;
- Destroys the joy of the family structure through confusion, chaos, strife and planting seeds of iniquity; and he
- Kills the joy of the family structure through death of a love one

satan attacks my Health System

In December 2012, after working a stressful year, it was time to take vacation as I usually did in prior Decembers so that I could return in January powered up and ready to go. During the last two weeks of 2012, I came down with flu-like symptoms, that is, the usual body aches and pains so I sought medical treatment to get relief. When 2013 rolled in I did not fully recover so I went back to the doctor to get to the bottom of my concerns. Various tests were done but they all came back negative.

From January to March 12, 2013, I continued my usual routine which included working hard, exercising, eating a balanced and healthy diet and having some fun with my family. I really was having a ball. In addition, at work I was selected to attend a one week credit union regulator's training seminar in California tentatively scheduled for April 8-14, 2013.

Our family decided earlier in the year, that we would initiate the process of securing electronic passports so by this time, I had secured all of our passports and was now in the process of ensuring that I had a US visa to travel to California. On March 13, 2013, I was scheduled for a follow-up visit with my doctor to continue the probing process of identifying what the problem was. However, my meeting that Thursday conflicted with another appointment that was work related, so I needed to reschedule my appointment to the following week.

On Friday evening, March 14, 2013, I felt tired so I did not accompany my wife to the food store as I normally would. On Saturday morning, I felt a lot better so I got up and did my usual chores and then I took my son to the computer store as promised and then paid a few bills. When we returned, I decided to lay down because I did not want to disappoint my wife again since we normally spent our weekends together.

When I awoke, after a few hours of rest, my wife had returned from the hair salon. I was wrapped up in a blanket because I had the same flu-like symptoms that I had during the previous Christmas—I experienced cold chills but had no nasal discharge. My wife said, "You do not look well in your face," and then indicated that she needed to take me to the doctor.

Then it happened to me

In the emergency room I was patiently waiting for the results of my blood test to determine the root cause of my flu-like symptoms. Then it happened to me. The doctor informed me that the white blood cell count for a male should range from 5,000-10,000. In my case, my white blood cells totaled 90,000. I was advised that I needed to be admitted to the hospital to sort out what was going on inside of me.

Later that day my wife and I received a courtesy visit from the oncologist who informed us that from the preliminary lab work it appeared that I had leukemia. In addition, we were also advised that in order to confirm the severity of the preliminary prognosis, further testing would be required, which involved undergoing a bone marrow biopsy. The following day a bone marrow was done and the sample was sent to the United States of America for analysis. In the meantime, I waited patiently for the results to get confirmation on my diagnosis. And what I was about to learn, changed my life in significant ways.

Motivational Quotes

- Focus on The One who can fix the problem.
- In the spiritual realm, a termination is considered a promotion.
- If satan attacks our economic system and we allow him to get away with it, then we will become his prostitutes.
- satan will attack our family structure.
- satan will attack our economic system.
- satan will attack our health system.
- If God allows the sickness, we have to take the test.
- Submit to the process of taking the test with the divine hope of passing it.

Motivational Scriptures

- "For God has not given us the spirit of fear, but of power, and of love, and of a sound mind" (II Timothy 1:7).
- "Now the Lord is that Spirit: and where the Spirit of the Lord *is*, there *is* liberty." (II Corinthians 3:17b).
- "I say unto thee, Arise, and take up thy bed, and go thy way into thine house" (Mark 2:11).
- "And whatsoever ye shall ask in my name, that will I do, that the Father may be glorified in the Son. If ye shall ask any thing in my name, I will do it" (John 14:13-14).
- "Be careful for nothing; but in everything by prayer and supplication with thanksgiving let your requests be made known unto God. And the peace of God, which passeth all understanding, shall keep your hearts and minds through Christ Jesus." (Philippians 4:6-7).

CHAPTER 2
WHERE IS GOD?

His Presence is from everlasting to everlasting

Around 2:30am, I was awakened from a dream. In the dream I was on a housetop preaching the Gospel of the Lord Jesus Christ in a rundown community. The atmosphere appeared to be very demonic as I descended from the housetop in a super-natural way. Then as I was walking through the neighborhood, the devil tried to instill the fear of death in me to discourage me from doing the work of the Lord. I saw a man staring me down with a high-powered, semi-automatic gun in his hand. As we were passing each other, I heard myself praying in the Spirit. I kept repeating "In the name of Jesus". Then I was immediately awakened from my sleep.

Anytime we experience fear, or a level of testing that we are unfamiliar with, our initial response, for the most part, is always directed at someone or something. How many of us stop to think for a moment that the test that has come may not be from God? Yet we convince ourselves that it is God anyway. In addition, we fail to stop and pull away from the test to identify its source. And before we even realize it, we conclude that it was God who sent it, when, in fact, the devices that were being used against us were coming from another source. God is not an evil God that sits on His throne to orchestrate evil upon His children. This is definitely outside the character of God.

Don't play the blame game

Many of us often use God as a scapegoat when we do not understand the test, the trial or tribulation, or even the source of the dilemma that we are faced with. If we have high blood pressure, we often blame the devil for giving it to us before checking our family history, our poor eating habits, the lack of exercise, being overweight, and most definitely our high cholesterol driven by the food choices we fail to give up. We give the devil too much credit and applaud him for things that he has no association or affiliation with. In fact, the blame game is often associated with our level of ignorance on the subject matter. The prophet Hosea said it plainly, **"My people are destroyed for the lack of knowledge"** (Hosea 4:6a).

However, **most of the tests that we will encounter in our lifetime will be driven or perpetrated by the devil;** and we should clearly recognize when we are being tested by him. **The devil's tests always subtract from our lives—they never add to it**. And if his intention is to add to or increase it always comes with a price tag that has a long-term negative impact on our walk and commitment to God. **"These things I have spoken unto you, that in me ye might have peace. In the** world ye shall have tribulation: but be of good cheer; I have overcome the world." (John 16:33).

When we blame God for our dilemma, it is a clear indication that we do not have an intimate relationship with Him or we do not know the character of our Heavenly Father. God does not have to send negative, life-threatening experiences to get our attention so that we can blame Him for them. However, He will use those experiences to get the glory from them.

> **"For every one that asketh receiveth; and he that seeketh findeth; and to him that knocketh it shall be opened. Or what man is there of you, whom if his son ask bread, will he give him a stone? Or if he ask a fish, will he give him a serpent? If ye then being evil know how to give good gifts unto your children, how much more shall your Father which is in heaven give good things to them that ask him?" (Matthew 7:8-11).**

Lips wide shut

It is not easy to keep our lips wide shut. However, **it is so easy to speak and entertain the spirit of condemnation** over our lives when we are tempted or are being tested in an area that seeks to stretch our faith in God. Some of us, like Job, curse the day that we were born. Some of us go into insanity mode and act out our frustrations and do things to those we love that we later regret. Nevertheless, I remember as clear as day when the doctor came into my hospital room and told my wife and I that the preliminary results indicated that I was diagnosed with acute myeloid leukemia (AML). I did not utter a word. **No, I was not**

in shock! I did not have a heart attack. I also did not think I was invincible.

However, I realized in that moment that the best thing for me to do before I responded was to do the right thing. **I kept my lips wide shut** because if I had responded in the natural realm, I would have allowed the physical man to go on the defensive and I would have begun swearing at God and His Kingdom, blaming everyone, including the dog and the cat, for my dilemma.

> **"Even so the tongue is a little member, and boasteth great things. Behold, how great a matter a little fire kindleth. And the tongue is a fire, a world of iniquity: so is the tongue among our members, that it defileth the whole body, and setteth on fire the course of nature; and it is set on fire of hell. But the tongue can no man tame; it is an unruly evil, full of deadly poison"** (James 3:5-6, 8).

This was a perfect opportunity for me not to allow the physical man (that is, the emotional side and weak side) to dominate the spiritual man, who should always be the dominating portion of my being. How could I respond in this way? It took all of the God in me to keep my faith and strength so that I could focus on my Source, the God I serve. If I had allowed myself to fall apart then it might have been the beginning of my downfall as a believer. There was no time to allow the flesh to have its way. **"For to be carnally minded is death; but to be spiritually minded is life and peace"** (Romans 8:6).

However, **I did not allow the doctor's report to enter my spiritual man**; it simply allowed me to quietly purge the doctor's report and rebuke satan's death sentence over my life. I knew without a shadow of a doubt that God did not send sickness in my life to take my life; but I believed that He would use this sickness to increase my faith and get the glory from it.

When we do not keep our lips wide shut **we have the power to condemn ourselves by the negative words we speak. "Death and life is in the power of the tongue: and they that love it shall eat the fruit thereof" (Proverbs 18:21).** When satan was allowed to test Job, he too, for a period of time, spoke condemnation on himself. He said, **"Man that is born of a woman is of few days and full of trouble" (Job 14:1).** When we think about it, this statement seems to have significant relevance to the tumultuous situation that Job experienced. Even his friends, Bildad, Zophar and Eliphaz condemned Job because they believed that he had done something wrong to experience so much trouble. They did not keep their lips wide shut when they should have done so. Job had to pray for them so that God could forgive them for their sin. We should practice keeping our lips wide shut especially when we are frustrated. This will help us to avoid planting negative seeds that can contaminate our environment.

Remember God's protection is with us

satan cannot enter our lives whenever and in whatever manner he wants to. Individuals who believe otherwise need to realize that is a lie from the very pits of hell. God our Father is not just going to drop us off at satan's daycare and leave us to be annihilated and abused by demons. **God has our back**, and He has had it before the foundation of the world was created. **Remember, God's protection is evident in three areas of our lives as believers.** One, **God has a hedge of protection**

around us that cannot be penetrated unless He gives satan permission to enter our lives. satan said, "Hast not thou made an hedge about him, and about his house, and about all that he hath on every side? thou hast blessed the work of his hands, and his substance is increased in the land." (Job 1:10). This means that God has released angels of protection upon us; they are responsible for our protection. God has released angels to protect our homes, properties, and our environment. God has also released angels to protect our wealth. Two, remember, God has a hedge of protection on our personal health. "And the Lord said unto satan, Behold all that he hath is in thy power: only upon himself put not forth thine hand. So satan went forth from the presence of the Lord" (Job 1:12). Three, remember, God has a hedge of protection over our lives. "And the Lord said unto satan, Behold, he is in thine hand; but save his life" (Job 2:6).

Remember God allows the Test

It is true that every test that we experience in our lives is not of God. Some tests are a result of the bad decisions we make or fail to make; and therefore, the test comes to put us back on the right track. If a husband who is in agreement with his wife allows her to continue spending money faster than he can make it, both of them will soon discover the consequences. The husband will be tested to bring his wife's spending under subjection. His test will continue until he passes it, or he will soon discover that his house will come financially tumbling down. The wife will be tested in spending restraint and money management. She will take this test until she learns how to exercise priority spending.

Some tests are designed to make us stronger, to go from faith to faith and glory to glory. Other tests are sent from the very pits of hell. Oh yes, the devil will test us also. Whether we want to believe it or not some of the devil's tests are designed and orchestrated to take us out of this world, but only if we give him that authority over our lives. Every test that satan tries to implement, he must first get permission from God to implement it.

"And the Lord said unto satan, Hast thou considered my servant Job, that there is none like him in the earth, a perfect and an upright man, one that feareth God, and escheweth evil? Then satan answered the Lord and said, Doth Job fear God for nought? Has not thou made an hedge about him and about his house, and about all that he hath on every side; thou hast blessed the work of his hands, and his substance is increased in the land" (Job 1:8-10).

The good news is God allows it for one purpose only. **satan has already been defeated before the foundation of the world was created**. This means that the battle has already been won, and we must now walk in the manifestation of that victory. He tries anyway even though he knows he is defeated. But he tests us anyway hoping that we walk in defeat and not in victory.

We should never allow ourselves to become discouraged when we are being tested by satan simply because God allows the test; and **if God allows the test, we can have confidence that we will be victorious**. In addition, whatever plan satan initiates, that plan does not have the power to kill us as believers. In other words, satan's plan can never kill us because God has already spoken and satan does not have the power to kill what God has created. satan does not have any power. He acts like a roaring lion, but is not a lion. The only power he has is the power we give him. He is powerless without our permission and our authorization. He is only a spirit looking to take over our house. More importantly, satan is an illegal being on earth as he does not have a physical body to operate in. He is not a roaring lion, but sounds like one in an attempt to instill fear in us and demonize our lives. "Be sober, be vigilant; because your adversary the devil, as a roaring lion, walketh about, seeking whom he may devour" (I Peter 5:8).

Where is God?

Whether we are being tested by God or satan, it sometimes feels like God is on vacation. This is normal because we feel like our world has caved in on us. Actually, this is one of the characteristics of God that I did not get until now. All of my life I have been taking tests and never once stopped to ask myself the ultimate question, 'Where is God? I know that God is in Heaven and His presence, through the Holy Spirit, resides on earth. However, the revelation is, all of my life I have been reading and studying God's Word, but now comes the test. And where is God? Answer: He is right there in the test. How do I know? All of the tests that I have taken (the easy and the difficult ones) during the past 36 years, the tester (who is the Holy Spirit) never left my presence. Have you ever taken a sit down test and then saw the teacher and your mentor leave the room? Of course not! The Teacher always stays until the test is over. The mere fact that the Holy Spirit shows up to the test should give us the confidence to take the test because we know that He will be there for us until the test is over. He shows up to give us encouragement, strength and the capacity to pass the test according to the Father's divine purpose and will for our lives. **"And I will pray the Father, and he shall give you another Comforter, that he may abide with you for ever"** **(John 14:16).**

Motivational scriptures that confirm where God is in times of testing:

- "But none saith, where is God my maker, who giveth songs in the night; who teacheth us more than the beasts of the earth; and maketh us wiser than the fowls of the heaven?" (Job 35:10-11).
- "For it is God which worketh in you both to will and to do of his good pleasure" (Philippians 2:13).
- "God is our refuge and strength; a very present help in trouble" (Psalm 46:1).
- "The Lord of hosts is with us; the God of Jacob is our refuge. Selah" (Psalm 46:11).
- "Whither shall I go from thy spirit? Or whither shall I flee from thy presence? If I ascend up into heaven thou art there: if I make my bed in hell, behold, thou art there" (Psalm 139:7-8).

Motivational Quotes

- Most of the tests that we will encounter in our lifetime will be driven or perpetrated by the devil.
- The devil's test always subtract from our lives—they never add to it.
- It is so easy to speak and entertain the spirit of condemnation.

- Do not allow the doctor's report to enter and overtake your spiritual man.
- We condemn ourselves by the negative words we speak.
- satan cannot enter our lives whenever and in whatever manner he wants to.
- God has our back.
- God has also released angels to protect our wealth.
- God has a hedge of protection on your personal health.
- God has a hedge of protection over our lives.
- Remember, God allows the test.
- satan has already been defeated before the foundation of the world was created.
- If God allows the test, we can have confidence that we will be victorious.
- satan does not have the power to kill what God has created.
- satan does not have any power.
- He is powerless without our permission and our authorization.
- satan is an illegal being on earth.
- The Teacher always stays until the test is over.

CHAPTER 3
THE GOD DECISION

A Wise Man Trusts God in all of his Decisions

No one knows when we will be asked to make the God decision for someone we care about. When that opportunity arises it is imperative that we find the strength, wisdom and leading of the Holy Spirit to help us make that decision. The decision may be convoluted by the complexities of the situation that is taking place. It may also be contaminated by the level of critical care that is needed. However, a decision must be made; and that decision should not be made with a sense of procrastination. In most instances there is a small window of opportunity to address the matter head on. If no immediate action is taken, the potential exist to lose that person all because we were not aggressive and proactive in the process of getting them timely medical attention within reason.

Initially, the warning signs were not apparent to me. I just thought I had the flu and the treatment I was receiving was for the common flu. I just totally missed all of the warning signs. But I was always tired from working hard and burning the candle at both ends. However, looking back in retrospect, I do remember climbing the stairs and feeling somewhat tired, but this was nothing out of the ordinary because I was always somewhat exhausted after climbing two flights of stairs, particularly when I was carrying a laptop and my heavy computer bag.

My personal experience may not seem to be a hell wrenching story of deliverance to some of us, but to me I was in a place where I needed God to deliver me and move expeditiously on my case. God, who knows the end of everything before it begins, had mercy on me for the Lord Jesus interceded on my behalf.

My oncologist was taken aback at my condition and was amazed that I was still alive. How could someone who had been diagnosed with acute myeloid leukemia walk around in this state? Since I had not gotten immediate medical attention, I was told that I was a walking time bomb, and that it was just a matter of time before my body would react and launch into self-preservation mode.

One may not want to think about it but the reality was there. From December 2012 to March 2013, the possibility of having a stroke and/or a heart attack was very real for me based on my unknown medical condition. I could have been driving my sons to school and had a stroke. I could have been sitting in my office at work or even talking to my wife and had a heart attack. God kept me and preserved me because this was not His plan for me or my life. **The 'should be' did not make it to the possibility, and the possibility did not become a reality. In essence, I am a living miracle because God kept me.**

The Wrong Environment

For some reason or the other, I did not feel at home when they transferred me to the Intensive Care Unit, even though they tried to make me feel at home. I remembered clearly how they struggled to find one of my veins for intravenous purposes. It took about four nurses to find it, causing my level of discomfort to rise to an all-time high. At the time I was not convinced that I was getting the necessary care that I thought I should be getting because the caregivers seemed so casual in their approach when dealing with my situation. I felt like I was on my own—just me and the good Lord. While in the Intensive Care Unit, my recollection is far and wide in the sense that I do not even recall how long I was there; all I could recall was that I needed help but I was in the wrong environment to get it.

Mastering Procrastination

Mastering procrastination is very important when a decision has to be made regarding the management of a loved one's health. We take it for granted and leave all of the decisions to be made to healthcare professionals without adequate communication and collaboration. However, all of the decisions that are made are not always made in the best interest of the patient. For some healthcare providers, it is the bottom-line that comes first. I believe that when families are faced with situations like the one I experienced, there is a need for them to play a very active role in the decisions that are made. Often, people enter the hospital and the doctors cannot advise the husband or the wife regarding what the problem is or what steps are being taken to address and/or isolate the problem. In such a case, the family needs to have the tenacity and the boldness to start asking the hard questions in the best interest of the patient or their loved one. **When we master procrastination we maximize the potential of enjoying our loved ones in the future.** We minimize the risk and put ourselves in a position to make informed decisions regarding their medical condition.

The Preacher and my Wife

I am told by my wife that after I was transferred to the Intensive Care Unit, there was a need to reduce the number of visitors to my bedside because it appeared that things had taken a turn for the worse. Many of my family and friends, who came to see me, were not allowed in due to the nature of my preliminary diagnosis. This was done in my best interest and more so because I had developed pneumonia, experienced difficulties breathing and was in critical condition. My wife had to make a hard decision to limit the number of persons coming to see me to minimize my exposure level to infection. I am told by one of my colleagues who had come to see me that only the preacher and my wife was allowed to see me.

Do It Quickly!

On Tuesday, March 19, 2013, my wife was patiently waiting to see the lung specialist and to be informed regarding my condition. This was a critical time because my wife wanted to hear what the lung specialist had to say as well as pick-up my son from school within the same time frame. There was definitely a time conflict. However, she waited patiently for the specialist.

Finally, the doctor came and told my wife that, based on his preliminary assessment, things were not looking good for me. He said, **"Whatever you intend to do, do it quickly."** He continued his conversation with her and again said, **"Whatever you intend to do, do it quickly."** Then as he was leaving, he turned around for the final time and said, **"Whatever you intend to do, do it quickly."** Later, my wife advised me that when the doctor made that comment three times, she had heard God talking to her, and so her instructions were clear.

The God Decision

All of us are faced with decisions that we have to make in life; some are straightforward and others are very difficult. When we make a decision that is not based on having the right information or on legitimate research, it will definitely affect the outcome. **All of our decisions should include God, the God who sees and knows all things. "Trust in the Lord with all thine heart; and lean not to thy own understanding. In all thy ways acknowledge him and he shall direct thy paths" (Proverbs 3:5-6).**

The worse decision is no decision at all. How many of us seek God's direction even when we have to make decisions that affect our loved ones? How many of us are guided by our emotions? In my diagnosed situation, it would have been normal to leave me in a local hospital and wait to see what the test results would be one week later. However, my wife knew that she had to urgently make a decision in my best interest. Her decision was made based on the leading of the Holy Spirit. She called this decision, "the God decision" because God was leading the process that would result in my receiving medical care outside

The Bahamas. My wife immediately submitted to the process and began to execute "the God decision". My passport was at the US Embassy in Nassau, for a US visa, awaiting pick-up so that I could travel to California for the one-week training for regulators.

Later, I am told by my wife that, as she was leaving the hospital, one of the nurses asked her, "Are you okay?" And she responded, "Yes." She also advised the nurse on duty that she wanted her husband air-lifted as soon as possible. Then she saw the charge nurse and told her to call the oncologist to advise him that she wanted her husband air-lifted that day. She also secured my passport from the U.S. Embassy, and had a flight chartered from Nassau to Miami.

Around 11:00pm March 19, 2013, I was air-lifted and admitted to a US hospital in Miami, Florida-Emergency Room. **It was a "God decision"**. If my wife had decided not to obey God by having me air-lifted one day later or whenever she'd decided it would be a good time to do so, she might have been singing the song, **"I will meet you in the morning someday"**. But praise be to God, she decided to do it when she did, and for this I'll be forever grateful to God and her. When God speaks to us we must not second guess His voice; but be led by the Holy Spirit. **"My sheep hear my voice, and I know them, and they follow me" (John 10:27)**.

Motivational Scriptures

- "Thy Word is a lamp unto my feet and a light unto my path" (Psalm 119:105).
- "In all thy ways acknowledge him, and he shall direct thy paths" (Proverbs 3:6).

- "I have taught thee in the way of wisdom; I have led thee in right paths" (Proverbs 4:11).
- "But the path of the just is as the shining light, that shineth more and more unto the perfect day" (Proverbs 4:18).

Motivational Quotes

- When we master procrastination we maximize the potential of enjoying our loved ones in the future.
- The 'should be' did not make it to the possibility, and the possibility did not become a reality.
- All of our decisions should include God, the God who sees and knows all things.
- The worse decision is no decision at all.

CHAPTER 4
TO HELL AND BACK!

God's Presence is everywhere

Most of the people who are admitted to the emergency room have some ailment or condition that requires immediate medical attention. I was in a crisis and the fight of my life. I remembered being rolled off the chartered plane and placed in an ambulance headed for hospital's emergency room. During the ride I knew that the Holy Spirit's presence was strong with me. I did not fear for my life, but I felt the fear of the Lord. I am told that when I came in, I was in pretty bad shape because I was about to go into respiratory failure.

The last thing I remembered was lying in a dark and cold room with my brother, Wellington, waiting to be registered. I am told by my wife that the doctors had to look down into my throat (a process called endoscopy) to determine what was going on before they could stabilize me and address my condition. Even though the risk was high, they assessed the situation and, taking the risk, they determined that they had to take a look. When I awoke, I had spent nine days in the Intensive Care Unit. I was being treated for pneumonia, viral and fungal infections which had attacked my body.

Down into Hell I go

As my body began to respond to the treatments being provided, it was time for the doctors to address the main reason why I had come to the hospital from The Bahamas. I had experienced many tests, trials and tribulations in my life, but none compared to the hellish experience that I went through as I battled acute myeloid leukemia. Persons who are diagnosed with leukemia have many treatment options. My treatment option was chemotherapy. The first eye opening experience was that I had to sign a living will giving my wife the power of attorney to make medical decisions on my behalf in the event I was unable to. This was intimidating but not a frustrating experience because I knew in whom I believed, and the God of my soul was watching over me. **"The Lord is my light and my salvation whom I shall I fear? The Lord is the strength of my life; of whom shall I be afraid?" (Psalm 27:1).**

I will never forget April 03, 2013 for the rest of my life. This day coincided with the same day we celebrated "Good Friday", the day we commemorated Jesus' death on the cross. There, He paid the ultimate price for the sin of all mankind. This was the day I started my chemotherapy treatment. My introduction to chemotherapy was called, "the Induction Process". This process was what I considered to be my introduction to hell. Doctors prescribed a seven-day/three-day chemotherapy regimen for me. Seven-day/three-day meant that I would receive one chemo drug for seven days. Also, for the first three days I would receive another chemotherapy drug consecutively. I was given two potent chemotherapy drugs called, Cytarabine and Daurnorubicin. The potency of these drugs were very high which posed life threatening possibilities for me. If this is the road that I have to take to recover from this disease then I would travel this road. I will travel it because God is on this road with me. **"The Lord will strengthen him upon the bed of languishing: thou will make all his bed in his sickness" (Psalm 41:3).**

The following are some of the major side effects of the chemotherapy:

- Pain;
- Low blood counts;
- Extreme nausea
- Vomiting
- Severe loss of appetite
- Intolerance to the smell of food;
- Loss of taste for certain foods;
- Muocitisis;
- Uncontrollable diarrhea;
- Skin changes;
- Heart problems such as slowing down of the heart beat and pumping function of the heart;
- Severe drop in blood pressure.

The Valley and the Shadow of Death

When I started the chemotherapy treatment my white blood cell count was at 104,000 cells, which is considered extremely high.

For the next seven days my total white blood cell count was destroyed and my bone marrow, which held all of these cells, was totally wiped-out. I not only experienced the toxicity level of the poisons, but I was also down in hell. Every day I would count the number of bags that I had to endure; it was a very painful process that placed my body under serious duress. I certainly had a deeper appreciation for the words Jesus spoke after His resurrection. He appeared to His disciples and said, **"They shall take up serpents and if they drink any deadly thing, it shall not hurt them: they shall lay hands on the sick and they shall recover"** (Mark 16:18)

Being in the valley of the shadow of death felt like someone had come and drained all the life out of me. It was a time of serious prayer and consecration with God. It felt like jumping out of a plane without a parachute. There were days when it felt like I was going to die. It also felt like my days of torment would never end. Then I remembered God's Word which says, **"Yea though I walk through the valley of the shadow of death, I will fear no evil; for thou art with me; thy rod and thy staff they comfort me"** (Psalm 23:4). My white blood cell count was totally wiped-out which meant my immune system was not able to provide protection against infection. This also meant that I was at risk for bleeding or hemorrhaging. I was also at risk for viral and fungal infections. I was required to go on an antibiotics regime (Fluconazole, Bactrim, Acyclovir and Levaquin (Levofloxacin). In other words, I was at the mercy of God.

Into the Pit of Hell I go

After the seven days of chemotherapy, and through no fault of my own, I developed mucositis resulting from a low white blood cell count that develops in the mouth, a side effect of the chemotherapy. The mucositis had damaged the tissue in my throat and also affected my ability to swallow. **This was a horrifying experience, which I would not wish on my worse enemies.** The pain from the mucositis gravely affected my ability to think clearly and have peace of mind. **It was like an excruciating pain from another world.** For about **ten days** I could not talk effectively, consume food, or swallow my saliva, and it was a hell wrenching experience to drink fluids. I was very miserable, uncomfortable and found it extremely difficult to communicate with my wife who was with me during this period. I had to use signs and pointed at things while she did most of the talking.

I could not swallow my saliva or water, and dared not even bother trying to eat food. Thank God for intravenous fluids that provided fluids to my body. Every day I would look forward to eating but was unsuccessful. I was salivating so profusely that I had to use a suction machine for at least three days (24/7) to get some relief from the uncontrollable levels of saliva production. The doctor had also prescribed a **magic mouthwash** which I used to wash my mouth; and was supposed to help me swallow daily. This, however, did not provide me with the relief I really needed.

The agonizing pain continued so I was prescribed morphine which I had never had before in my entire life. Many say that when someone is prescribed morphine the pain obviously is unbearable. The dosage of morphine prescribed was like **"eating candy"**. It did not provide me with any level of comfort or pain relief. The doctor then prescribed a morphine pump. This morphine pump was placed on a six-minute timer. My wife and I laugh about it now but it was serious business when I was using it. The pain was so bad that every six minutes I was like a drug addict waiting for **"his hit"**, the moment to press the morphine pump. Even while I was sleeping throughout that first day, my wife pumped the machine for me. **"For thou wilt not leave my soul in hell; neither will thou suffer thine holy one to see corruption (Psalm 16:10).**

Eventually, I made up in my mind that the best thing for me to do was to come off the pump for two reasons. One, after I had finished using the pump, the possibility existed that could result in another problem for me, becoming addicted to morphine. Two, the pump did not bring total relief from my pain. But I had made the decision that I would "take it like a man". It sounds like a crazy thing to do, but I was looking at the big picture. Over the ensuing days, the pain started to subside and my tolerance for the pain became bearable.

I was just There

You may think that after all of my hell wrenching experiences or troubles, the worse would be over! Wow! Was I in for the surprise of my life! While in hospital, around 5:00am-6:00am every morning, the nurse would come and take blood from me and send it to the lab for the doctors to assess my progress. Then the news would be revealed when the team of doctors came to make their rounds. They told me that I would need platelets, potassium, and/or magnesium, so when I had to get one unit of blood, it would take two and a half hours, and an additional half hour for pre-medication. If my potassium levels were low, it would take about an hour maximum. The worse part of this experience was whenever I needed potassium, I would feel like a dead man. I would have no energy. It appeared as though my total body, including my muscle functions, froze because I could not move. I was just there—yes, I was just there waiting for my change to come. It was not until I received my transfusion of potassium that I would feel normal again and carry out my regular activities. I did recognize that even in the midst of this experience that God's hand of protection was keeping and restoring me. In other words, **when we are in the weakest hours of our lives, God's presence operates at its optimal level. "He giveth power to the faint; and to them that have no might he increaseth strength" (Isaiah 40:29).**

I'm Back... the Resurrection

It is amazing how much the human body can tolerate even when it is under attack. My body was under severe attack! It seemed that this level of hell would never end; but, thank God, it came to an end. The good news about bad experiences, relationships, pain and the devices of the enemy is, it is not going to last forever. **"Weeping may endure for a night, but joy cometh in the morning" (Psalm 30:5b).** I am back because God has a purpose for my life.

Even though I was in the pit of hell during my chemotherapy treatment, **I was determined to come out as pure gold**, because I was confident that God would not leave my soul in hell. **"For thou has delivered my soul from death, mine eyes from tears, and my feet from falling" (Psalm 116:8).** The chemotherapy was over and now I must begin the process of rebuilding my faith and physical strength in the Lord. During this experience, my wife would say, "Bertie, I am like your coach, to get you back in the game."

More than Conquerors

When we, as believers, go through the storms of life, we should not suffer from an identity crisis. We should know whose we are and who we are. Yet, there is a tendency to go with the flow or downplay our circumstances. Sometimes we even pretend that we have it together but in reality we do not. I believe that **during our darkest hours we should shine the brightest because we know that God has our back. We are victorious through Christ our Savior and Redeemer**. Despite our situation, **God has already empowered us with the capacity to overcome whatever life pitches at us.** We have already been sworn into God's Kingdom so we are entitled to all of its benefits. **"Bless the Lord O my soul and forget not all his benefits; who forgiveth all thine iniquities; who healeth all thy diseases" (Psalms 103:2-3).**

In addition, **we are kings in a kingdom of kings.** This also means that we often have to go to war to protect our territory or environment that the enemy will try to infiltrate. This should not stress us out; and we should not be surprised when satan comes to go to war against us, whether it is a war against our bodies, our finances, our families or it is a strategy that he seeks to use in an effort to dominate an area of our lives. There is no doubt about it, **we have to take a stand and go to war, in the spirit, against that devil**! I am also confident that my big Brother, Jesus, who is the King of kings, has already defeated the devil before the foundation of the world was created. **He has also given me the power and the authority through His Word to overcome any battle that rises up against me.**

"Who shall separate us from the love of Christ? Shall tribulation, or distress, or persecution, or famine, or nakedness, or peril or sword? As it is written, for thy sake we are killed all the day long: we are accounted as sheep for the slaughter. Nay, in all these things we are more than conquerors through him that loved us" (Romans 8:35-37).

Motivational Scriptures

- "Jesus said unto her, I am the resurrection and the life; he that believeth in me though he were dead, yet shall he live" (John 11:25).
- "For thou wilt not leave my soul in hell; neither will thou suffer thine holy one to see corruption" (Psalm 16:10).
- "And he said unto me, My grace is sufficient for thee: for my strength is made perfect in weakness. Most gladly therefore will I rather glory in my infirmities, that the power of Christ may rest upon me." (2 Corinthians 12:9).
- "Behold, God is my salvation; I will trust and not be afraid: for the Lord Jehovah is my strength and my song; he also is become my salvation" (Isaiah 12:2).
- "God is my strength and power; and he maketh my way perfect" (2 Samuel 22:33).

Motivational Quotes

- When you are in the weakest hours of your life, God's presence operates at its optimal level.
- I was determined to come out as pure gold.

- During our darkest hours we should shine the brightest.
- God has our back.
- We are victorious through Christ our Savior and Redeemer.
- Despite our situation, God has already empowered us with the capacity to overcome whatever life pitches at us.
- We are kings in a kingdom of kings.
- He has also given me the power and the authority through His Word to overcome any battle that rises up against me.

CHAPTER 5
MAN IN THE MIRROR

The Glory of the Lord is everywhere

When man was in the Garden of Eden he had it made in the shade. Everything was provided for him and he was given total authority over all the earth. He had total control of how he looked in the mirror. However, through his free will and disobedience he contaminated the perfect picture that God had given him to reflect on. **Adam changed the man in the mirror**. Instead of being an original in the mirror, he reflected an image that was outside the perfect will of God.

Instead of God destroying the reflection of the man in the mirror, He provided an escape for him so that he could become an original image in the mirror of life again. God did not become stressed out, nor did He flip off the handle like some of us do when things go array or when we are disappointed. He just went into redemption mode and implemented His plan to save man to return him to his original position in the mirror of life.

Today, man no longer has to avoid the mirror; he can now stand boldly in front of the mirror and, not only declare the blessings and promises of God on his life, but also see and live the real man in the mirror.

The old Man in the Mirror

Physically, the battle had begun in earnest between my old and new body. In the old body, the pain and suffering was unbearable but this was inevitable. What happened? Doctors had to literally kill the old man through a process of "induction" chemotherapy so that the old man could never be resurrected from the dead again.

For three weeks, while I was in the hospital, the old man in me died physically because of the intense trauma and process that he had experienced. The doctors had to empty my bone marrow by killing all of the diagnosed leukemia cells. Then, they performed a bone marrow biopsy to make sure and/or measure the level of diagnosed leukemia cells that were or were not present in the bone marrow. **Every morning they performed an autopsy on the old man to make sure that he was dying or was dead.** When Christ was crucified, and died, on the cross the soldiers had to ensure that He was dead.

> **"But one of the soldiers with a spear pierced his side, and forthwith came there out blood and water. And he that saw it bare record, and his record is true: and he knoweth that he saith true, that ye might believe." (John 19:34-35)**

They killed me with my eyes wide open. The old man was crucified and buried so that the new man could come alive.

Protection from Depression

Sometimes it is the small things that we take for granted when we are in the valley of testing, such as protection from depression. It is normal human behavior for persons, who have been diagnosed with acute myeloid leukemia, to go into depression. Some view it as a death sentence. **But I viewed the diagnosis as receiving a new lease on life**. After all, **I would not get any brownie points, move to the head of the class or receive a purple-heart medal for going into depression**.

Even though going through the seven days of chemotherapy was hell wrenching, at no time did I feel depressed or entertained it in my mind. I knew that the angels were protecting me, and that the presence of the Holy Spirit was encamped around me. **"Thou will keep him in perfect peace whose mind is stayed on thee; because he trusted in thee"** (Isaiah 26:3).

Everyone needs protection, especially from depression. We are also admonished never to walk around with mental or emotional baggage because God knows the impact on us when we carry the extra load on our physical and mental faculties. Such a load would definitely send us into depression; and **depression can often lead to despair and self-destruction**. The Bible declare:

- "Come unto me all that labor and are heavy laden, and I will give you rest. Take my yoke upon you, and learn of me, for I am meek and lowly in heart; and ye shall find rest for your souls. For my yoke is easy and my burden is light" (Matthew 11:28-30).

- "Cast thy burden upon the Lord, and he shall sustain thee: he shall never suffer the righteous to be moved" (Psalm 55:22).
- "Casting all your care upon him; for he careth for you" (1 Peter 5:7).

Protection from negative Environment

When we are in the valley of the shadow of death one of the most important things to remember is, **we must protect our environment from negative influences.** It is so amazing that when we are down how satan conveniently sends his representatives to contaminate our environment and plant seeds of hopelessness and despair. satan will also try to plant the seed of death there. However, we and our loved ones must protect our environment from negative influences because it can adversely affect us physically and psychologically. It is vital that we keep our environment a positive and hopeful one. If we know family members who are negative, then we should at most try to manage those interactions.

If there's one thing I'm grateful for it is that God protected me by not allowing some of my family and friends to come and see me during my induction period. No, they are not all negative influences, for the most part, but if they had seen me in the state that I was in, they probably would have been unable to retain themselves, and thus, contaminate my environment. Thanks be to God who protected my environment from family and friends. **"He that dwelleth in the secret place of the Most High shall abide under the shadow of the Almighty"** **(Psalm 91:1).**

Of course, some of us complain that some of our family members do not visit us in the hospital or when we are going through our valleys. And why is this so? The answer is obvious. God is protecting us from some of them. He is also protecting us from being concerned about people who are not concerned about us. Isn't it a blessing that while we are down that we do not have to fight additional battles? We need to remember these profound words of Scripture: **"And we know that things work together for good to them that love God, to them who are the called according to His purpose" (Romans 8:28).**

I saw a glimpse of Death

The last time I looked in the mirror was March 15, 2013, the Friday morning before going into the emergency room. Often, I would spend time in the mirror ensuring that I was well groomed before leaving the house. After my seven-day chemotherapy sessions, I felt the need to look in the mirror. My wife did warn me that I should not look in the mirror because I might not like what I see.

However, I wanted to look anyway, although I was not intentionally ignoring the counsel of my wife. I had to look because I wanted to see how I looked after the chemotherapy sessions to know what impact it had on my face. **When I looked in the mirror I was staring at a total stranger**. I could not believe my eyes. My face was half its size after I left The Bahamas. My head had major patches as if someone had randomly removed large clusters of hair from it. My complexion was extremely dark, almost the color of a newly paved road. I almost went into an anxiety attack, because I could not believe my eyes. I looked closely again and realized what I had seen.

I looked as if I had seen a ghost. My face was as if someone had come by with a vacuum machine and took a suction hose and reduced my face to half of its current size. I saw a glimpse of death, and it was not a good picture. So the best thing for me to do at the time was to pull myself together because, if I did not, I may have overreacted in the flesh and possibly sinned. Thank God I didn't respond to my flesh! I found comfort and encouragement in knowing that when Christ comes back for us we will have a body that cannot be destroyed or that will never die. **"For we know that if our earthly house of this tabernacle were dissolved, we have a building of God an house not made with hands, eternal in the heavens" (2 Corinthians 5:1).**

The Man in the Mirror

After looking into the mirror the revelation hit me that God had allowed me to look this way as part of the process of killing the old man. Jesus came to kill the old man; and this is how I should look when the old man is dying inside of me. **Until the old man dies, the new man in the mirror cannot come forth and have dominion over his entire past (which included being diagnosed with leukemia).** It was a shocking experience to see myself like that in the mirror; but I did not realize it then that was the way I was supposed to look for a short period of time.

The day I was discharged I looked at the man in the mirror again. What did I see? I saw a new man, a manifestation of God's miraculous handiwork in action. I looked like a new creature as God had promised. Is it possible for me to be resurrected without physically dying and being placed in a grave? Oh yes! This process is called healing. **When God heals us He actually kills only the disease portion of us without destroying our entire physical man. The scapular is the Word of God and the anesthesia is the Holy Spirit providing comfort throughout the seamless process** (A supernatural process to remove the disease out of our lives permanently, destroying the cause of the problem we call sickness). He does this and replaces only those organs, cells or body parts that were affected.

When I came to the hospital three months ago, I was diagnosed with leukemia, and these cells, doctors say, were dominating and controlling various functions of my body, preventing it from operating normally. Things that I could not do three months ago, I can do them now. For instance, I had a serious problem with breathing on my own. My lungs were severely affected which made it difficult for me to breathe freely without the assistance of an oxygen tank. I am now able to breathe and walk for miles on my own.

When Jesus saves us from our sins, He saves us and heals us through the power and anointing of His Holy Spirit. **"Therefore, if any man be in Christ, he is a new creature: old things are passed away; behold all things are become new" (II Corinthians 5:17).**

Characteristics of the old Man

- Doctors prescribed cholesterol medication.
- Doctors prescribed Diovan, Adalat and Lazix blood pressure medication.
- Weighed up to 274 pounds in 2011.

Characteristics of the new Man

- Doctors prescribed a very low dose of blood pressure medication due to the chemotherapy treatment.
- There was no need for further cholesterol medication.
- My current weight now stands at 228 pounds.
- My faith is much stronger than before.

It is so easy to give up when we look at ourselves in the mirror of life. However, we must be assured that it is not God's intention for us to live in a mirror that does not reflect his image and his likeness. We should strive to be the man in the mirror that Jesus was while he was on earth.

Motivational Scriptures

- "Let this mind be in you which was also in Christ Jesus" (Philippians 2:5).
- "And be not conformed to this world, but be ye transformed by the renewing of your mind, that ye may prove what is that good, and acceptable, and perfect, will of God" (Romans 12:2).
- "For as in Adam all die, even so in Christ shall all be made alive" (I Corinthians 15:22).
- "And so it is written, the first man Adam was made a living soul; the last Adam was made a quickening spirit" (I Corinthians 15:45).

Motivational Quotes

- Adam changed the man in the mirror.
- They killed me with my eyes wide open.

- The old man was crucified and buried so that the new man could come alive.
- Everyone needs protection, especially from depression.
- Depression can often lead to despair and self-destruction.
- We must protect our environment from negative influences.
- Until the old man dies, the new man in the mirror cannot come forth and have dominion over his entire past.
- When God heals us He actually kills only the disease portion of us without destroying our entire physical man.
- The scapular is the Word of God.
- The anesthesia is the Holy Spirit providing comfort throughout the seamless process.

CHAPTER 6
THE GOD RESPONSE

A Wise Man waits for God to give him Directions

When a house is on fire, it does not matter who calls 911, but the call is made so that the fire department can respond to the fire. Once the call is made, the fire department has a responsibility to respond to ensure that they are carrying out their mission as a fire department. When they arrive, the fire marshal has to quickly assess the situation and use all of his resources to put the fire out. It is satan's role to bring the fire of hell into our lives as his mission is to totally destroy our faith in God, and he hopes that the fire will also destroy us in the process.

As children of the Most High God, it is God's responsibility to deliver us from the fire when we cry out to Him. It is unthinkable for the God of the universe to sit on His throne and hear the cries of His children and refuse to take action. We can argue the point that God allowed the children of Israel to suffer 400 years of slavery in Egypt even though they cried out to Him for help. This is true; however, God did answer their prayer in the fullness of time.

> **"And it came to pass in process of time, that the king of Egypt died: and the children of Israel sighed by reason of the bondage, and they cried, and their cry came up unto God by reason of the bondage. And God heard their groaning, and God remembered his covenant with Abraham, with Isaac and with Jacob. And God looked upon the children of Israel, and God had respect unto them" (Exodus 2:23-25).**

God hears our prayers for help and responds in three ways: He either says, "Yes, no or not now." The 'not now' response is the answer most of us do not want to hear especially when we are in the valley of the shadow of death or when we feel as though we are at the end of our rope. Nevertheless, God being the God who knows the end of everything before it begins **always responds in our best interest.** The bottom-line is, God is concerned about everything that happens to us, including those things that have the potential to affect our walk with Him.

Invoke the Covenant

In every relationship there is a mutual understanding between both parties; and each person in the relationship has a responsibility or a commitment to do certain things to maintain that relationship. God is also this way because He is a covenant keeping God. He honors all of His commitments despite our imperfections. **God keeps His commitments to** us not just because He is God but because His Word demands no less.

One of the fascinating characteristics about God is that He does not go around flexing His muscles or trying to impress us like men do to impress women. Remember our first new credit card and the excitement of wanting to go to the mall and shop till we drop? We have access to the credit card, but we cannot use it until the card is activated by the credit card company. God is not going to activate certain portions of His covenant in our lives until we cry out to Him for help. **We need to call on God to activate the benefits He has promised us in His Covenant**. This may seem elementary but God wants us to call on Him; after all, **He is our Helper. "Call unto me, and I will answer thee, and shew thee great and mighty things, which thou knowest not" (Jeremiah 33:3).**

Daily confess His Promises

Our healing also comes through our confession of God's promises. We are admonished to speak those things that become sound doctrine. **Daily confession of God's promises is critical to our faith in God.** It is critical because confessing God's Word not only increases our faith, but also increases our confidence in God. **"Now faith comes by hearing, and hearing by the Word of God" (Romans 10:17). "But without faith it is impossible to please him: for he that cometh to God must believe that he is, and that he is a rewarder of them that diligently seek Him" (Hebrews 11:6).**

When we daily confess the promises of God over our lives we change the atmosphere and our circumstances. We fill our internal and external environment with the presence of the Lord. This also reminds God of His commitment to not let His Word fall to the ground and on deaf ears. This also allows **the Word of God to come alive and penetrate our shadow of death experiences. "Bless the Lord O my soul and all that is within me, bless his holy name. Bless the Lord O my soul and forget not all his benefits: who forgiveth all thine iniquities; who healeth all thy diseases" (Psalm 103:1-3).**

- "For I am the Lord that healeth thee" (Exodus 15: 26b).
- "But He was wounded for our transgressions, he was bruised for our iniquities: the chastisement of our peace was upon him; and with his stripes we are healed" (Isaiah 53:5).

The God Response

After being in the hospital for about three weeks and experiencing hell wrenching moments, I needed a God response. A God response would give me the strength to go to the next level in my life. I needed to be ministered to and I desperately needed to hear a Word from the Lord. It is a wonder how God will show up in our lives when we least expect it. God has a way of hearing and answering our prayers before we have the opportunity to go into panic button mode. Definitely, God is an awesome God **who sends His angels to minister a Word to us in so many ways.**

- **God sends His Word**

Around this time, which I perceived to be one of my darkest hours, that is, after experiencing significant side effects from the chemotherapy, God sent His Word to me. While lying in bed and having a casual conversation with my wife, the Word of the Lord came to me. The Word said,

> "But now thus saith the Lord that created thee, O Jacob and he that formed thee O Israel, Fear not: for I have redeemed thee. I have called thee by thy name; thou are mine. When thou passest through the waters, I will be with thee; and through the rivers, they shall not overflow thee: when thou walkest through the fire, thou shalt not be burned; neither shall the flame kindle upon thee" (Isaiah 43:1-2).

Immediately I knew that God had heard my prayer. This answered prayer signified that God had this situation under His control so there was no need for me to worry, display any level of stress and/or start pulling my hair out. Even though I had to go through the process, (the fire and the water), God was right there in the midst of it with me.

- **God reveals His Word**

After being discharged from the hospital, I felt as strong as an ox. I took a trip home to The Bahamas to see my sons and daughter but was advised by my doctors that I had to come back for further treatment to ensure that the diagnosed leukemia would remain in remission. As I continued to walk in God's divine authority and blessings, I was re-admitted into the hospital to do my first round of **"consolidation"** chemotherapy. This round is called a 1-3-5 chemotherapy treatment. This meant that they would administer chemotherapy over a five-day period on days one, three and five. The dosage was called **Cytarabine**.

It was during this period that I decided to study the Word of God. In all of my life, this particular scripture verse in Isaiah never stood out to me before; and if I had read it before, I was probably too busy trying to get through the book to pay close attention to it. As I read Isaiah, the Lord revealed to me this verse: **"Then shall thy light break forth as the morning, and thine health spring forth speedily: and thy righteousness shall go before thee: the glory of the LORD shall be thy rereward"** **(Isaiah 58:8)**. I was in awe because this was the second time in a very short period that **God had sent healing and deliverance through His Word**. To God be the glory!

• **Vision of the Donor**

After being discharged from the hospital where I completed my first round of consolidation, the wheels were in motion for me to undergo another round of 1-3-5 "consolidation" chemotherapy. I would have to spend another week in the hospital and wait an additional three weeks before my cell counts would begin to normalize. In the meantime, plans were also being made for me to have a **stem cell transplant**. The type of stem cell transplant that I would be getting is called, **"Allogeneic stem cell"** transplant. **This means that my brother or sister who is a match with my DNA would be extracted by a machine and their stem cells will be infused to me in a process similar to me having a blood transfusion.**

Coming from a big family, and based on the fact that we had the same mother and father, I had eight brothers and three sisters who were potential donors. Doctors say that, for every four siblings, there is a 25% chance that one of them would be a match.

So the bigger the family, the greater the chances. I did not sit down and try to determine which of my brothers or sisters would be the perfect match because I knew that God was in control, so I sat back and let him reveal to me the chosen one. As one of my sisters and I were having a conversation, I remembered her giving her personal opinion as to which of my eight brothers would be a match, and thus, become the donor. She chose my ninth brother who was two years younger than me. She also chose two of my other brothers who were one and two years older than me respectively. In fact, all of us were waiting patiently to see which one of my brothers would be a match. When God told the prophet Samuel to go to the house of Jesse to anoint the next King of Israel he was given specific instructions.

> **"But the LORD said unto Samuel, look not on his countenance, or on the height of his stature; because I have refused him: for the LORD seeth not as man seeth; for man looketh on the outward appearance, but the LORD looketh on the heart. And Samuel said unto Jesse, Are here all thy children? And he said, There remaineth yet the youngest, and behold, he keepeth the sheep. And Samuel said unto Jesse, Send and fetch him: for we will not sit down till he come hither. And he sent and brought him in. Now he was ruddy, and withal of a beautiful countenance, and goodly to look to. And the LORD said, Arise anoint him: this is he" (1 Samuel 16:7,11-12).**

Our vision of who the donor would be and God's vision of who he would be were totally different. As a matter of fact, the two donors whom God chose was never on my sister's list. They were not even close to her "guesstimation" of choices. This is how awesome God is. The news was in. God chose my eldest and fourth eldest brothers who carried blood and tissue matches like myself. One of my brothers is in his sixties and the other is in his mid-fifties. The point is they were a perfect match. My fourth brother Wellington was the chosen donor and God looked at his heart; he is very outgoing and have what I consider to be "happy cells." My two immediate big brothers who were one to two years older than myself are very strong, robust and goodly to look upon. However, God knew why He did not choose them.

God knew who the donor would be before the foundation of the world, because He knew that the devil would make an attempt to take my life. I never understood why God blessed my mother with twelve living children. I must admit, I was totally ignorant. This revelation has totally blown my mind! I realize now that my mother, who was a praying woman from I was a child, not only submitted her life to the Lord but was also obedient in submitting her body as a living sacrifice. Now when I see a mother with a lot of children, I can now say to her, **"Woman, you are blessed of the Lord and highly favored!"**

Motivational Scriptures

- "Who his own self bare our sins in his own body on the tree that we, being dead to sins, should live unto righteousness: by whose stripes ye were healed" (1Peter 2:24).
- "And Jesus went about all Galilee, teaching in their synagogues, and preaching the gospel of the kingdom, and healing all manner of sickness and all manner of disease of the people" (Matthew 4:23).

- "But when Jesus heard that, he said unto them, They that be whole need not a physician, but they that are sick" (Matthew 9:12).
- "And he said unto her, Daughter, be of good comfort: thy faith hath made thee whole; go in peace" (Like 8:48).
- "He shall call upon me, and I will answer him: I will be with him in trouble; I will deliver him, and honor him. With long life will I satisfy him and shew him my salvation" (Psalm 91:15-16).
- "Hear my cry O God; attend unto my prayer. From the end of the earth, will I cry unto thee, when my heart is over-whelmed: lead me to that rock that is higher than I" (Psalm 61:1-2).
- "In my distress I cried unto the LORD and he heard me" (Psalm 120:1).
- "Hear my prayer, O LORD, give ear to my supplications: in thy faithfulness answer me, and in thy righteousness" (Psalm 143:1).

Motivational Quotes

- It is God's responsibility to come to our rescue when we cry out to Him.
- God hears our prayers for help and responds in three ways: He says, "Yes, no or not now."
- God always responds to our prayers.
- God always responds in our best interest.
- God is a covenant keeping God.
- God activates His covenant in our lives when we cry out to Him for help.
- Our healing comes through our confession of God's promises.

- Daily confession of God's promises is critical to our faith in God.
- Daily confession increases our faith and confidence in God.
- Daily confession changes our atmosphere and circumstances.
- The end result of prayer is a God response.
- God sends healing and deliverance through His Word.
- When we daily confess the promises of God over our lives we change the atmosphere and our circumstances.

CHAPTER 7
ANGELS WATCHING OVER ME

A wise man depends on God for supernatural protection

Who would have thought that I would find myself registered as a patient in a local hospital in The Bahamas? Who would have thought that amidst everything that is positive going on in my marriage, my family and my close knit regulatory team, that a man like me would have to put his life on pause? Well, this is how life sometimes throws us a curve ball; but this does not mean that we have to accept the pitch. We all have choices and we are governed by our choices based on how we respond to the curve balls in our lives. There is a need for even me, a boy raised in the ghetto, who has been serving God most of my life, to continually request divine protection. This protection I pray for everyday as I plead the blood of Jesus over my family, wealth, home, and wherever I go, as well as for my safe return home. Oh yes, I believe that angels are watching over me.

To me, it was no surprise that the enemy had chosen this particular time to attack my life because he knew that just a few years ago I had taken a stand and written a book called, "Kingdom Empowerment-Principles to Living An Empowered Life". satan thought that I would be like him and suffer from Alzheimer's disease and forget what I had said in that book; and now his attack was supposed to have a devastating impact on me. satan realized that it was time to put my walk with God to the test, because I knew myself, and had publicly declared an all-out war on his kingdom. After serving God for more than 36 years of my life, I had decided that it was too late for me to backslide, too late to waste my life on just existing, and too late not to draw a line in the sand. I was determined to chart the direction of my life going forward. I believed that the best thing for me to do at age 47 was to recommit my life to the Lord and engrave a sign on my tabernacle that says, **"Sold to the highest bidder before the foundation of the world was created"**.

However, satan actually believed that he had a right to occupy and take up residence in my body. Therefore, I had to go through the process and live by the standard (the Word of God) that God had set for me from the beginning. This meant that the pressure was not on me, but on God to fulfill His Word and refine me like pure gold in the process.

satan tried to kill me softly

On Saturday evening, March 17, 2013, after being admitted, I was assigned to a semi-private room? While the room was okay, they had assigned me to a bed that was in the corner of the room, next to an air-conditioning unit. From the time I was admitted into the emergency room, up to the time I entered my semi-private room, satan went into full gear to put his plan into action. Experiencing shortness of breath at the time, I did not take this action lightly. Why would someone who has been diagnosed with leukemia complain anyway? After all, I was cold, shaking and feeling very weak at the time.

Everyone who knows Bert Mullings will tell you that I am not a complainer, and definitely not a pushover. However, I was compelled to do something. I knew it was the Holy Spirit discerning my situation, bringing it to my attention so that I could raise a "red flag" (a trap of the enemy). I knew without a shadow of a doubt that it was the right thing to do. I complained under the authority of the Holy Spirit that resides in me, making my petition known very quickly and diplomatically. **"For the weapons of our warfare are not carnal but mighty through God to the pulling down of strongholds" (2 Corinthians 10:4).** I said to the attending nurse, "Why in the world would they put me next to an air-conditioner knowing my diagnosed condition?" I demanded that the hospital authorities find me another room or switch my bed accommodations with the other patient in the room.

satan's plan, in hindsight, was to shut me up quietly by putting me next to the air-conditioning unit to further escalate my problem and shut my system down before anyone noticed what was happening. **His plan of trying to kill me softly failed because angels were watching over me** to give me the protection I needed through my insight to avoid the trap of the enemy. **"No weapon formed against thee shall prosper and every tongue that shall rise against thee in judgment thou shalt condemn. This is the heritage of the servants of the Lord, and their righteousness is of me, saith the Lord" (Isaiah 54:17).**

I got worse

Many of us are of the opinion that when we are admitted to the hospital for treatment or care that we are safe and the scare is over because everyone is working on our behalf to get us better. Well, if we believe this we are clueless and ignorant of the fact that everyone is not working on our behalf. I remember a friend of mine telling me that **the hospital is also the devil's playground.** We cannot accept everything at face value. We have to question those providing the care and become a part of our healing process.

Okay, we would think that since satan's plan of action failed that he would just leave me alone. You guessed it right! He did not leave me alone. As a matter of fact, he did just the opposite. He turned up the heat. I am told that the disease moves very quickly in adults who are diagnosed with leukemia. In the emergency room, I was diagnosed as having 90,000 white blood cells, and two days later the cells were still increasing. On Monday night the doctor ordered that I have a blood transfusion. The doctor did not communicate this to me or my family, so how would we know that I needed blood immediately?

satan used this information by working in his representatives so that I would not be given the blood I needed. I got worse! During this time, I became weaker not only because my white blood cells were high, but because I needed blood to give me the energy to fight back. I was also given Nebulizer treatments to control my breathing and to keep my lungs open. One of my close relatives, who came to see me, said, "I came to see you and you were sleeping; but it looked like it was hard for you to breathe. I did not want to wake you so I allowed you to continue sleeping."

I knew that God was with me because He dispatched an angel to my rescue to **deliver me from satan's second attempt on my life**. The nurse that was assigned to me realized that I was getting worse. The nurse knew that I was supposed to get a blood transfusion that the doctor had ordered, but satan's representatives refused to give me one unit of blood. I am told that the nurse pleaded with the supervisor until I was given the blood that I needed.

Angels of Escalation

God sends angels of escalation in our lives to put us in an environment that prevents certain events from taking place in our best interest. When my nurse, who is my angel, saw that I was getting worse, the second goal was change my environment. satan's plan was to finish me off once and for all. Around 4:00am Tuesday morning I was awakened out of my sleep by the nurse who was divinely sent into my room to put the devil to open shame; the nurse advised me of the situation. The nurse said, "Mr. Mullings, you are getting worse and we are moving you to the Intensive Care Unit." I immediately went into action and called my wife and advised her of the situation. **My first line of defense was to call for back-up.** This is something most of us do not do when we find ourselves in the valley of the shadow of death. This, however, was not my doing; but it was the Holy Spirit directing me, and I submitted to His directives. **"Be not forgetful to entertain strangers: for thereby some have entertained angels unawares" (Hebrews 13:2)**. To God be the glory!

Angels of Direction

God sends angels of direction in our lives to get us to a specific destination so that we can be in the right place at the right time to meet our appointments with destiny. Even though I got worse, there were no plans or discussions to escalate my intensive care status to another level. God, who knows the end before the beginning, dispatched an angel to my rescue to bring my wife the message that it was time for me to get medical attention somewhere else. The lung specialist, who was not the primary health care provider, was sent to speak directly to my wife for such a time as this. He could have spoken to her two, three or seven days later. However, this was not the case. He spoke to her in a timely manner. This was the time when I was at my weakest point in the local hospital. The lung specialist words were direct, to the point and required my wife to take immediate action. He said, "Whatever you do, do it quickly." This is how I knew that God had sent him when He did because on my file at the hospital in the USA it said that I was about to go into respiratory failure when I arrived. The angel of direction was working on my behalf to get me to a specific destination. To God be the glory!

> **"And when they were departed, behold, the angel of the Lord appeareth to Joseph in a dream, saying, Arise, and take the young child and his mother, and flee into Egypt, and be thou there until I bring word: for Herod will seek the young child to destroy him (Matthew 2:13).**

Angels of Protection - Event I

God sends angels of protection in our lives to provide personal security and safety as we go through our valley experiences. I remember, clear as day, that while in hospital, my blood pressure level was lower than usual. It was like around 101/50 after the nurse's assistant came and checked it. The nurse was about to give me my pressure medication when I was compelled to challenge her. I said, "Your assistant took my pressure about an hour ago and the reading was 101/50, why are you giving me pressure medication after this reading? Is not that going to drive my pressure too low?" I have discovered throughout my experience that when a person's pressure is low, there is no need to give them blood pressure medication. Based on my past experiences, my blood pressure usually drops about 20-30 points when medication is prescribed based on the effects of the chemotherapy. This means **my diastolic** (bottom number) would drop from 50 to 20. Obviously, she failed to check the chart and reviewed the last reading. My angel of protection was there to prevent any potential mishap on the nurse's part and, thus, relieved me of any negative and/or life threatening experiences. Thank God for angels of protection.

Angels of Protection - Event II

During the past three months, I have been through hell three times and back based on the levels of chemotherapy that was administered to me. The seven/three day chemotherapy treatments were the worse as I did experience some of the most hell wrenching days of my life. However, I knew that I was not alone because God was protecting me. When I was discharged from the hospital I was not carried out in a wheel chair; I walked out. This is what I call divine intervention for the angels of the Lord protected me throughout this entire process. I also had two series of one-three-five day (1-3-5) chemotherapy treatments which lasted over a five-day period. I did not have any side effects from these two experiences. I walked out of the hospital immediately after completing my treatments. This is God, keeping me and protecting my body, mind and soul after taking these poisons.

Angels of Protection - Event III

My wife and I went shopping after my last round of chemotherapy. We were having a great time with each other and the shopping experience was a time to do something different for a change because, while in hospital every day, I saw just a window and four walls. I guess you can imagine it's like being in prison. Of course, you can, and sometimes do, experience the feeling of being in a prison. But thank God for His Son, Jesus Christ, who can set us free. **"If the Son therefore shall make you free, ye shall be free indeed" (John 8:36)**.

As we were returning home, and when we were about one minute from our apartment, it happened. My wife's brother, who was driving, decided that he was going to cross over into the next lane and turn the corner to drop us off. It happened so fast! He did not see the on-coming car, and before we knew it, the car was about 20 feet away from us. Based on the speed of the car, and my position in the front right passenger side, I could have been hit and injured severely. However, the angel of the Lord intervened and protected me because the car did not hit us. He stopped abruptly just in the nick of time to avoid being hit by the oncoming vehicle.

At the time, my white blood cell count was almost zero, and my platelets were also very low. This meant that I could not take any type of bruising and/ or afford to be hit by a car, because this would have caused serious bleeding and clotting issues for me. This would be considered a perfect recipe for complications. **"For He shall give his angels charge over thee, to keep thee in all thy ways" (Psalm 91:11)**. Again, God had protected me as His angels of protection prevented this serious mishap.

Angels of Protection - Event IV

One week before I was about to go into the hospital to start the stem cell transplant process, I was given the green light by my oncologist to have my teeth assessed by an oral surgeon. When I finally saw the dentist, he advised me that I needed to undergo four extractions. I was like "you cannot be serious". Then I submitted and said, "I came this far, and I am not coming back again, so let's take all of them out now." On our way home, we had to stop at the pharmacy to fill the prescription. My wife carried one of the prescriptions inside but did not realize that each prescription was written on separate sheets of paper, so she left one in the car. The dentist prescribed **Motrin** pain medication—one of the forbidden pain medications that I could not have. The Holy Spirit prompted my wife about this as she realized that this was one of the medicines that I could not have.

Later that evening, I experienced bleeding until about midnight; then I stopped bleeding, so I went to bed. Around 2:00am I was awakened from my sleep, and to my surprise, my gums were bleeding heavily, non-stop. When someone is diagnosed with AML we are advised that if there is bleeding we should find the nearest emergency room because blood platelets are low and the risk of non-clotting is very high. We rushed to the emergency room where I learnt that my pressure was severely elevated, 147/107. Again, God's angels had protected me. I thank God for waking me up so that I could get the medical attention that I needed to stop the bleeding and reduce my high blood pressure (which is usually 101/55).

Angels of Protection Scriptures

- "The angel of the LORD encampeth round about them that fear him, and delivereth them." (Psalm 34:7).
- "My God hath sent his angel and hath shut the lions' mouths that they have not hurt me; for as much as before him innocency was found in me; and also before thee, O king, have I done no hurt" (Daniel 6:22).

Other Motivational Scriptures

- "Bless the Lord, ye his angels that excel in strength, that do his commandments, hearkening unto the voice of his word" (Psalm 103:20).
- "But to which of the angels said he at any time, sit on my right hand, until I make thine enemies thy footstool? Are they not all ministering spirits, sent forth to minister for them who shall be heirs of salvation?" (Hebrews 1:13-14).

Motivational Quotes

- I'm sold to the highest bidder before the foundation of the world was created.

- God sends angels of escalation in our lives to put us in an environment that prevents certain events from taking place in our best interest.
- God sends angels of direction in our lives to get us to a specific destination so that we can be in the right place at the right time to meet our appointments with destiny.
- God sends angels of protection in our lives to provide personal security and safety as we go through our valley experiences.
- Always call for back-up.

CHAPTER 8
I'M STILL HERE

Unmovable faith shall be rewarded

On July 2, 2013, I was sitting in the waiting room to see my stem cell doctor. I was fortunate to have met many doctors since my stay in hospital over the past four months. One of the doctors who was treating me said, "You are a miracle of medicine." For a moment it sounded like he was making a good statement. Medicine did play a role. After all, he is a doctor and I had to excuse him for about 10 seconds. Why? Because I had to accept the fact that this is what he was trained to say based on my medical history and his personal observations.

His statement was a good statement, but it was not the right statement. I responded, "I am a miracle! I am a **miracle of the Living God of Abraham, Isaac and Jacob. I am a miracle of Jehovah Rapha -The Healer**." If I had agreed with the good doctor, it would have nullified everything that God had done for me. I would be publically confessing that God was not a Healer and that this entire process was orchestrated by medicine and a team of educated doctors. There was no way that I could allow the devil in any form or fashion to snatch the glory that was due to God from my lips, and then put me in a corner to agree with a lie from the pit of hell.

When we are in the valley of the shadow of death, we should not under any circumstances allow the enemy to trick us into declaring a lie. We should not allow caregivers to believe that if they had not done what they did, then we as believers would not have the ability to testify of the goodness of the Lord. "**The Lord is my shepherd and I shall not want**" (Psalm 23:1). This means that all of my needs are met; and, because they are met, I lack nothing in any area of my life.

We must guard the doors and windows of our hearts from the enemy. We must control what goes into our spirit man so that we do not speak death over what God has already given life to. The enemy is very clever to use doctors and practitioners to make us believe that they are responsible for our healing, a virtue that only comes from God. I am not surprised that they will speak this way, but I cannot agree with their belief systems and teachings. If I allow it, before I know it, I would be confessing, "I am a miracle of medicine"; and when the medicine fails me, I would be back to where I started all over again. I would be on the verge of respiratory failure. I would be diagnosed again with acute myeloid leukemia. I would then have to take three rounds of chemotherapy again with no hope for healing because I believe in the medicine and not in the God of the medicine. **And again my response is, the devil is a cross-eyed liar!**

Celebrate God's goodness

When the Miami Heat won the 2013 NBA championships all of the team members were excited. We saw and felt the excitement of how it feels to be champions even though many of us were simply fans of the winning team. In the stadium, even fans, who were pulling for the opposing team, congratulated the Miami Heat for winning the championship. During the entire celebration, none of the team members focused on how many games they had lost, or how hard it was for them to win any of their season games. No one complained about how many of the team members could not play due to injuries encountered during the season. The team celebrated their win by pouring champagne on each other, hosting parties and celebrating with the public by having a public parade.

God demands from us and wants us to celebrate His goodness. We limit God by only celebrating when things, events and life are going in the right and up direction. Many of us only know God in the good times; and it is so easy to trust Him when it does not cost us anything or when there is no crisis in our lives. This does not require us to have any faith in God. When things are not going well, the first name we call on is Jesus. However, we do not see or feel the need to celebrate the God's goodness when things are not going well. The problem is, we allow our emotions to control our spirit man and we start having pity parties or playing the 'blame game'.

The devil does not want us to celebrate the goodness of the Lord. He wants us to cry our eyeballs out and blame everything that is happening to us on God. However, **we must become "party animals"**, like the world and celebrate God even if we do not have anything to celebrate. We must celebrate in the midst of our storms. We must celebrate when we are in the fire, the rain, and when we are in the valley of the shadow of death. When the doctors give us a report that is a death sentence we must celebrate the goodness of God.

If we ask unbelievers why they are having a party, most of them will tell us that they are having it because it feels good to have a party. If we want to take a stand in our situation and let the devil know that **"we are still here"** then we have to take God at His Word and execute His Covenant.

> **"Make a joyful noise unto the Lord, all ye lands. Serve the Lord with gladness: come before his presence with singing. Know ye that the Lord he is God: it is he that hath made us, and not we ourselves; we are his people and the sheep of his pasture. Enter into his gates with thanksgiving and into his courts with praise: be thankful unto him, and bless his name. For the Lord is good; his mercy is everlasting: and his truth endureth to all generations" (Psalm 100:1-5).**

Don't live in the past

Living in the past can have a devastating impact on how we respond to our current and future circumstances. My response, based on the reports of the doctors, will determine whether I accept their reports or whether I allow those reports to cripple my faith going forward. Many of us who have been diagnosed with a disease find ourselves confessing what the doctors say. Even though it may seem that it is okay to say what the doctors have said, the reality is, we are inviting that spirit of dis-ease to manifest itself not only in our lives but also to take up residence in our environment. **"Neither give place to the devil" (Ephesians 4:27).**

During my entire experience, there was never a day that I confessed that I had any type of disease. Doctors, nurses and administrative personnel would ask, "What is your sickness?" I would say, I was diagnosed with acute myeloid leukemia; and not I have acute myeloid leukemia. I never confessed and/or declared any sickness over my life. Sickness is a spirit; and if I confess that spirit over me, it will come over me seeking to control my life. All of the doctors and persons I came into contact with would say, "You look like there is nothing wrong with you." They would also say, "Why am I here because you look great!" The reason they can say this is God has totally and completely heal me; and my daily confession was that I am not living in the past. I am not living my life based on what the doctors say that I have. I am living my life based on the present and my future. What were/are some the **scriptures and words of encouragement that I said/say to speak life over myself?**

- "Then shall thy light break forth as the morning, and thine health shall spring forth speedily: and thy righteousness shall go before thee; the glory of the LORD shall be thy reward." (Isaiah 58:8)
- "I am healed and delivered."
- "I am totally and completely healed before the foundation of the Lord was created."
- When people ask me, "How are you doing?" My response would be, "I am excellent; I am well."
- "God is good to me all the time."

- "I am blessed and highly favored of the Lord."
- "Bless the Lord and forget not all of His benefits; who forgiveth all thine iniquities who healeth all of thy diseases"(Psalms 103:2-3).

When we live in the past we are entertaining the spirit of sickness. This is what the devil wants us to do. He does not have a body to reside in, but if he can get us to live in the past he can live in our past (the place where our sickness resides) and then he can use our past to disrupt our present and our future. His goal is to keep us sick. If he keeps us sick, this allows him to continue living in our past, present and future. As believers we must live in the now (the present) and confess our healing into the future. **Do not let the devil make us prisoners of the past**.

Staying in the game

It does not matter what we are going through. More importantly, it also does not matter what inning it is in the game of life; for as long as we have the strength and determination to live, there is hope. The key is, in the midst of all of our past failures, **we have the power to stay in the game**. The choice is not that of our spouses or our children, we must make up in our own minds that this is the way forward and pursue it with a passion. **Staying in the game should be our number one priority**. Having a conversation with one of my brothers opened my eyes to a new revelation. No one who is diagnosed with a life threatening disease spends most of their time counting money and or focusing on their wealth. This is important but not a priority. I spent most of my time focusing on staying in the game and walking in victory; that was and is my priority.

After all of the pain and suffering that I experienced during my first round of chemotherapy, I had to pull myself together to stay in the game. Lying in bed was not going to contribute significantly to my walking out of the hospital. So, I initially started walking out of my room with a walker. A few days later, I was walking the hallway a few times; and before I knew it, I was walking about two miles every day. I was determined to walk out of the hospital and get to the next level. I decided that I was going to do everything within my power to have the doctors discharge me from the hospital. In fact, just before I was discharged from the hospital, one of the physical therapists gave me a nick name. He called me the Bahamian Ox.

No time for complaining & murmuring

It was so easy for me during my experience to develop and facilitate an environment of murmuring and complaining. This is one party I could start hosting without any effort. However, I intentionally and deliberately chose not to start it because I knew that the consequences would not be positive. During one of my hospital visits, I was fortunate to have listened to an interaction between a cancer patient and the doctor. The doctor asked one of the patients who was receiving chemotherapy, "How do you feel?" The patient responded, "Terrible, I feel awful!" I said to myself, no wonder you are having such a hard time with the treatment; you are spending too much time complaining about what is happening to you and not enough effort is being invested in the positive things that are happening in your life. She could have very well said, "I feel great, thank God for life. It's a miracle that I am still here today. Thank God for keeping me during this process. I feel terrible, but thank God I still know when I feel terrible." As long as we are alive, there is hope. As long as we have an opportunity to give thanks, let's give thanks, regardless of how we feel or the report that the doctors bring us. **Complainers never win; and winners never complain. It takes less energy to give thanks to God than it does to develop a strategy that facilitates complaints and allows us to keep on complaining about almost everything every day.**

After all I had experienced I cannot allow myself to start complaining or murmuring about what has transpired in my life. **Murmuring cultivates an ungrateful spirit.** It is worse than complaining because you can audibly complain under your breath, but murmuring takes it to another level. It drives me crazy to see children murmuring about things, especially when they ask their parents to go somewhere and their parents tell them no. They would display their level of dissatisfaction by moving their lips, but will not utter a word. It often appears as if they have a psychological problem. **Murmurers die in the process of receiving their blessings. "Neither murmur ye, as some of them also murmured, and were destroyed of the destroyer" (1 Corinthians 10:10).**

Time to change lanes

Throughout this entire experience, as I begin to look back on where God has brought me from, it has been very rewarding and mind-blowing. I was air-lifted at the outset and today, I am sitting in my condo writing about my experiences in this work entitled, **"Not Easily Shaken"**. Driving on the I-95 Highway again gave me a new perspective about life that I did not realize before. I saw four lanes. One lane was called the "Sun Express". In this lane we can arrive very quickly to our destination without the hassle of getting caught up in traffic and we only have minimum delays if there is an accident in this lane. Two, the other two lanes on the left are considered the fast lanes; they also have the potential benefit of getting us to our destination, but at the risk of incurring an accident. Three, drivers, who were in the lanes that were on my right, focused on driving at a reasonable speed and, if they needed to, they could quickly access the changing lanes to ensure that they have ease of exit to reach their final destination.

I realize that I'm still here because God, through this entire process, is constantly changing the lanes in my life to ensure that I reach my destination on time. He is also changing my lanes to ensure that I have ease of access to all of His benefits whenever I need them. **Without God it is impossible for me to reach my destination on my own merit. "The steps of a good man are ordered by the Lord: and he delighteth in his way" (Psalm 37:23).**

Keeper of my soul

None of us have all of the answers as to why some of us live and some of us die. It is my personal conviction that, it is God's Word and **our level of faith that drives us to our destination**. In other words, it is our faith that makes us whole. I could find a thousand reasons why I am still alive today and if I carefully orchestrate these reasons none of them could include God if I wanted them to. However, this does not mean that I am telling the truth; and this does not mean that God is not a part of the process. The point is, many of us take it upon ourselves not to include God in our lives and we try to resolve most of our problems and challenges without asking God for help. To the wise, this is suicide. How can we, with such limited power, rely on our own strength? **God is the ultimate solution to all of our problems.**

God is the Keeper of our souls. This is the one thing that we cannot put in a vault and use to increase the dollar amount in our savings account. Only God is endued with the power to watch over our souls. Despite our situation, that is, any situation that all of us have in varying degrees, we should put our lives on pause and acknowledge that God is here to assist us in whatever way we need Him to and to bless us in the process. I did not gamble at the lottery machine and got 'the prize' called sickness. I did not ask to be diagnosed with a disease to see how the experience would be and to suffer in the process. Nevertheless, in the process, I surrendered my life to God, the Keeper of my soul, asking Him to deliver me from this disease that had affected my immune system. I am here because God is the Keeper of my soul, and nothing can change that reality for me. This means if He is my Keeper, He will do everything in His power to bring about the manifestation of that healing into the physical realm. He cares so much for me that He healed me before the foundation of the world was created; and I know that He cares about the sanity and preservation of my soul.

> **"The Lord is thy keeper the Lord is thy shade upon thy right hand. The sun shall not smite thee by day, nor the moon by night. The Lord shall preserve thee from all evil: he shall preserve thy soul. The Lord shall preserve thy going out and thy coming in from this time forth, and even for evermore" (Psalm 121:5-8).**

Don't change your attitude

All miracles are initially manifested in the spirit realm. Then we see physical manifestations of those miracles now or in the future based on our faith. Jesus healed the blind man with his spit and mud. He was instantly healed, but he had to go and wash his eyes to see the physical manifestation of his miracle.

Even though we have faith in God and believe that God has healed us, our healing starts in the spiritual realm. We must not under any circumstances change our attitude towards our healing even though we do not instantly see the physical manifestation of our healing. God is working with us in the process to remove the dis- and give us the ease we so desire. Changing our attitude slows down the process, and if we continually change our attitude, it will come to a complete stop. Can you imagine the blind man failing to go and wash his eyes from the spit and mud after Jesus healed him? This would have resulted in an environment of doubt and he would have remained blind for the rest of his life. Having a positive attitude brings healing and restoration to the process. Every time someone asks me, "How do you feel?" One hundred percent of the time I would respond, "I feel excellent." This is not putting on a show! It is a declaration of my faith because if I believe that I have been healed before the foundation of the world, I have no dis-ease (no discomfort) even if the spirit of that disease appears to continue to reside in my body. We must declare with our attitudes that it is well with our souls. **"Let this mind be in you which was also in Christ Jesus" (Philippians 2:5).**

I'm still Here

The oncologist had said that I was like a walking time bomb, just waiting to explode based on the severity of my diagnosed condition. From all indications, it was just a matter of time before I would suffer a stroke or a heart attack. While in hospital in Nassau, I got worse and was transferred to the Intensive Care Unit. Then, I got worse again and my wife, based on a God decision, was prompted by the Holy Spirit to have me air-lifted to the United States of America to receive advanced and specialized treatment based on the doctors' diagnosis.

In addition, I spent significant time in recovery after being stabilized. Then I had to recover from a serious case of mucositis which initially involved taking high doses of morphine and ultimately being placed on a six-minute time released morphine pump to minimize the pain and suffering I had experienced after receiving initial chemotherapy.

Furthermore, I received a total of four rounds of chemotherapy and was infused with more than 24 bags of medication. I was also given more than 73 bags of intravenous saline solution. I spent many hours in the hospital and in out-patient care, receiving more than ten (10) blood transfusions, and more than seven (7) blood platelet transfusions. I have taken numerous prescription medications that they are too many to remember. After my transplant, I have taken an average of 900 pills per month. I have worked with more than eight teams of doctors that surrounded my bed each morning during my hospital stay. I had four teeth extractions at one time; I awoke from my sleep and had to be rushed to the emergency room for continuous bleeding. Sleeping for a full eight hours had become a luxury; I did not sleep normally for six months due to hospital sleep interruptions. I have spent more than two months on lockdown in the hospital and confined to my room.

Nurse visits totaled more than twenty (20) and they have extracted more than eighty (460) vials of blood to conduct laboratory tests to monitor the progress of my vitals and restoration of my immune system. I have been exposed to four bone marrow biopsies to analyze the status of my bone marrow (remission of the diagnosed acute myeloid leukemia).

I had two visits to the cardiologists which involved a stress test, lab works and tests to determine the strength and functioning of my heart. I also had an intense pulmonary test to test my breathing and lung capacity. I have also had more than five chest x-rays, two EKGs and one Echocardiogram test to observe the walls of my heart and to monitor my heart beats, etc. I have been on antibiotics to prevent fungal, viral and bacterial infections for more than six months. Additionally, for more than six months, I could not eat raw vegetables or consume certain fresh fruits. I have not sat in a restaurant for almost six months and cannot eat fast food due to the potential hygiene risks of attracting bacterial infections.

I know it sounds like someone is complaining; and it sounds like I am looking for someone to feel sorry for me. Absolutely and positively not! Nothing could be further from the truth! The point is after all I have gone through, I'm still here. I'm still here. Let me say it again, just in case it did not resonate in your spirit. I am still here! I could spend the rest of my life whining about everything that has happened to me and what I have experienced, but it will not get me to the next level in my life. My key focus today is doing whatever is necessary to pass the tests that I have to pass today. In other words, my faith in God is focused on powering me, no matter what comes my way, to be successful in achieving all of the goals and objectives of today so that I can please God.

The time has come for all of us not to waste our time focusing on and promoting the negatives of what has happened to us. We should focus on the positives. Yes, it hurt when I was diagnosed with AML, but **I did not allow the hurt** to **cripple me or my attack strategy to deal with what the doctors diagnosed.** Any disappointments in my life were not for the worse, they were for my good. Now, that's hard to swallow, but I swallowed it with the confidence that the Lord Jesus Christ have my back. When things do not go our way, this should let us know that God is protecting us for a reason, so all we need to do is be patient and see what the end of our delays will be. I am not going anywhere! **"I will not die, but live, and declare the works of the Lord" (Psalm 118:17).**

When we know what we know, we have the confidence to walk through the fire. When we know what we know, we have the confidence to believe God for a miracle and hold on to that miracle no matter what we see or what is happening in the physical realm. I am here because God is keeping me. I am here because God's Word cannot lie and God's Covenant, His Word, will never make a liar out of Him. I am here because of my faith in God, my Creator and Sustainer. Like the Apostle Paul said,

"For I am persuaded that neither death, nor life, nor angels, nor principalities nor powers, nor things present, nor things to come, nor height, nor depth, nor any other creature, shall be able to separate us from

**the love of God, which is in Christ Jesus our Lord"
(Romans 8:38-39)**.

Motivational Scriptures

- "Be still and know that I am God" (Psalm 46:10a).
- "For whatsoever is born of God overcometh the world: and this is the victory that overcometh the world, *even* our faith" (1 John 5:4).
- I have set the LORD always before me: because he is at my right hand, I shall not be moved (Psalm 16:8).
- He only is my rock and my salvation; he is my defense; I shall not be greatly moved (Psalm 62:2).
- Which holdeth our soul in life, and suffereth not our feet to be moved (Psalm 66:9).
- He will not suffer thy foot to be moved: he that keepeth thee will not slumber (Psalm 121:3).

Motivational Quotes

- We must guard the doors and windows of our hearts from the enemy.
- We must become "party animals".
- Don't live in the past.
- Do not let the devil make us prisoners of the past.
- We have the power to stay in the game.
- Staying in the game should be our number one priority
- Complainers never win; and winners never complain.
- It takes less energy to give thanks to God than it does to develop a strategy to complain.

- Murmuring cultivates an ungrateful spirit.
- Murmurers die in the process of receiving their blessings.
- Without God it is impossible for me to reach my destination on my own merit.
- Our level of faith that drives us to our destination.
- God is the ultimate solution to all of our problems.
- God is the Keeper of our souls.
- Do not allow the hurt to cripple me or my attack strategy.
- God is the Keeper of our souls.

CHAPTER 9
THE POWER OF BROTHERLY LOVE

A wise man sees beyond muddy waters

A king who feared God and humbled himself before Him told a parable to all of the children in his kingdom. He said, "For the kingdom of Heaven is like unto a king who served God most of his life and then fell ill. Everyone in his kingdom was shocked and concerned when they heard that the king was not doing well. His friends from near and far heard the news and also made inquiries as to how he was doing. As time went by, the king had to be sent far away to get the help he needed to deal with the problem that was affecting his ability to rule as king."

A girl asked, "Oh king, what happened to the king's family? Did they visit the king in his time of distress?" The king responded, "In the beginning, everyone was concerned about the king but only one of them went out of their way to see the king."

Another boy asked, "Was the king disappointed over the lack of support he got from his family and friends when they did not visit him?" The king responded, "It is very difficult when individuals are fighting for their lives because they very seldom get the level of support they need. I had to first forgive them for not coming to my rescue and use the strength that was available to me to fight back with all I had. If I had allowed myself to become bitter, it would have only poisoned the healing process."

The king continued telling his story. He realized that he needed true brotherly love to help him along the way. He was determined to find brotherly love so he wrote letters to some of his friends who made a commitment to help him. But he never heard from them as they were too busy in their own world and thought that his need was not important. The king was very disappointed but also realized that many people say they love you, but they do not display or have brotherly love. **"For I was an hungred, and ye gave me no meat: I was thirsty, and ye gave me no drink. I was a stranger, and ye took me not in: naked and ye clothed me not; sick and in prison, and ye visited me not" (Matthew 25:42-43)**.

God's undying love

For the Kingdom of Heaven is likened unto a king who was given authority and lordship over a territory of citizens. The citizens knew the laws of the kingdom but decided, through their own freewill, to do evil in the sight of the king. The king thought that if he enforced the law this would not solve the problem but make it worse; and then, all hopes of winning them back to him would be lost. So, despite their evil ways and lifestyles, he chose to love them. Even though they rejected him as their king, he continued to love them beyond boundaries. His love for them was unconditional to the point that the more evil they did, the more He loved them; and nothing they did or said changed His love for them.

How can we say we love someone when he/she continues to do evil, hurt our feelings and is totally aware of the damage that he/she is doing to us? Our first response would be to run and protect ourselves from the pain and suffering that the individual is about to place upon us. Only God can love us unconditionally and at this level. It can only be love that comes from another world (the Kingdom of Heaven). This is what God did. He chose to love us. He knew that if we did not have an escape plan we were on a direct collision course to hell; and it would be just a matter of time before we had an accident that would change the course and direction of our lives forever.

His undying love for us allowed Him to send His son Jesus to step into time and sit behind the wheel of life and take our place. It also allowed him to take on the burden and cost of all accidents before they happen so that we do not have to pay the eternal price for our sins. God's undying love gave us access to the greatest gift in His Kingdom, His Son, the Lord Jesus Christ. He spared nothing, including His Son, to win us back to Himself.

"For God so loved the world that He gave His only begotten Son, that whosoever believeth in Him should not perish, but have everlasting life. For God sent not his Son into the world to condemn the world: but that the world through him might be saved" (John 3: 16-17).

Christ's expression of true brotherly love

Many of us talk about real love but when the opportunity presents itself we are too selfish to fulfill that commitment or stand by the words we say. It is easy to donate a kidney or a piece of one's liver so that someone could live but to give our life so that someone else could live, that price is too high to pay. Why is this the case? Why haven't so many of us died so that some or all of us could live? Well, it is deeply rooted in the fact that we ourselves want to live and we do not have the power to give life.

Only the Giver of Life can give beyond a heart transplant and live. Only the Giver of Life can give beyond a kidney or liver transplant and remain standing after the process is completed, and, not only give one transplant, but as many as are necessary for as long as it is necessary.

When Christ came to earth He spoke of love and commanded us to love one another; and, He did not stop there. He took love beyond the power of infinity. He became the instrument whereby all men could find love and be loved. He demonstrated with His own life the ultimate expression of true brotherly love. Before He came to earth, he subjected himself to become the ultimate sacrifice. When He dwelt among us He physically showed us how much He loved us. **"Greater love hath no man than this, that a man lay down his life for his friends" (John 15:13).**

Brotherly love calls for sacrifice

When we face challenges and adversity, there is a level of expectation from those we love to provide a cushion of support that can be described as brotherly love. No one wants to feel as though he/she is being isolated, ignored and, even to a greater extent, in a world all by him/herself. After all, love is supposed to be the power mechanism that brings balance to the entire process.

However, when tragedy, trauma or adversity strike people know that support is required at some level or the other. But that support never comes because some of us put on blinders and chose to ignore the request to give brotherly love. We convince ourselves that helping, even in a small way, takes too much effort and is a distraction from doing the things that are so-called important to us. It is amazing how we have embroiled ourselves into a culture and environment of familiarity that when someone is down and needs our help we deliberately choose not to help them. This is not brotherly love.

Some of us, who have experienced tragedy, trauma and adversity, understand what some of us are going through, yet we take on a selfish attitude. We have clearly assessed the situation and know that we can help, but we refuse to do so. Some of us even go to the extent to make commitments to assist, but somewhere along the way shift gears and decide we are no longer prepared to assist in any way possible. We deliberately chose not to provide assistance because we do not have brotherly love.

Brotherly love calls for sacrifice. Many can raise their hands, volunteer or say how they can help, but unless a deliberate effort is made to do so, nothing will happen. We have to go out of our way to show brotherly love. **It demands that we find a way to help others. It means that we cannot show brotherly love by simply residing or remaining in our comfort zone.**

True characteristics of brotherly love requires the following:

- Putting another person's needs before our own;
- Assessing the situation and deciding how we can help;
- Following through on our commitments;
- Being prepared to mobilize our own resources;
- Having compassion before deciding to help others;
- Having mercy before we decide to help others; and
- Keeping our vows to help others.

The power of brotherly love in action

Six months ago, in the middle of the night, my fourth eldest brother, Wellington, left The Bahamas with me on an emergency flight to Miami, Florida to ensure that I was admitted to hospital. I was in Intensive Care Unit for about nine days, but I have very little recollection of the time spent there. I was very impressed with my brother because he spent all of his time sitting and sleeping on a hard chair, and making sure that everything went well during my period of crisis. In my opinion, I know it was rough because I find it very difficult to sit down for more than five hours without experiencing some level of discomfort.

When he was asked to volunteer to take me to the hospital in Miami, he dropped everything that he was doing at a moment's notice and made me his number one priority at the time. He sacrificed his personal time, business pursuits and his family of five, and left The Bahamas to assist a brother in need. When he realized that he had completed that mission, he returned home for a period.

Four months later, my brothers were tested to determine who was a match so that I could have a stem cell transplant. The results took about a month and many of them did not know who was going to be a match, or even that a match would be found. When the results were in, two of my brothers were a match. My eldest brother Frank and Wellington. I am told by my wife that when she asked Wellington to become my donor, he agreed right away, adding that he knew he was going to be my donor.

The Donor Process

Being a stem cell donor requires an extensive vetting process to ensure that the donor has the capacity to donate cells. It also means a two-week commitment by my brother to come back to the United States of America and undergo various tests and see various doctors. My brother came without hesitation and started the process. Some of the tests included pulmonary, an EKG, and an echocardiogram; he also had to undergo extensive blood tests, and assessments by a personal care provider. Then he had to see a specialist to secure the clearance he needed so that he could be approved to participate in the extraction of his donor cells. He subjected himself to this vigorous and transparent process. I was truly impressed with my brother because he never complained and displayed no fear or trembling during the entire process. He further subjected himself to taking **neupogen shots** to increase the growth of cells in his body. The potential risk included having severe bone pain that is out of this world. However, my brother was fixed on completing the process. Again, and, surprisingly so, he experienced no pain, and was as quiet as "a lamb going to the slaughter".

On the day of the stem cell transplant, my brother was placed in a room and connected intravenously in both arms to a machine that would facilitate and separate his white, red blood cells and platelets. He sat stationary for six hours, committing himself to the process. When he was finished, he contributed 9,000,000 cells and 5,000,000 cells were intravenously administered to me. He got up, laughed and walked out of the hospital, thanking God. This is truly amazing to me! To God be the glory!

Later, I realized that my brother did not have to give me his cells, but he did so willingly. I realized that he also could have agreed, and then, at the last minute said no; after all, this is something he had never done before in his life. Today, there is no doubt in my mind that this open display of my brother's concern for me was genuine for it has taught me the true essence of real brotherly love in action.

Motivational Scriptures

- "And the Lord shall guide thee continually, and satisfy thy soul in drought, and make fat thy bones and thou shalt be like a watered garden, and like a spring of water whose waters fail not" (Isaiah 58:11).
- "As the Father hath loved me, so have I loved you: continue ye in my love" (John 15:9).
- "Seeing ye have purified your souls in obeying the truth through the Spirit unto unfeigned love of the brethren, see that ye love one another with a pure heart fervently" (1 Peter 1:22).
- "There is no fear in love; but perfect love casteth out fear: because fear hath torment. He that feareth is not made perfect in love" (1 John 4:18).

- "Let brotherly love continue" (Hebrews 13:1).
- "But as touching brotherly love ye need not that I write unto you: for ye yourselves are taught of God to love one another" (1 Thessalonians 4:9).

Motivational Quotes

- Brotherly love calls for sacrifice.
- Brotherly love demands that we find a way to help others.
- We cannot show brotherly love by residing or remaining in our comfort zone.
- Brotherly love requires putting another person's needs before our own.
- Brotherly love requires assessing the situation and deciding how we can help.
- Brotherly love requires following through on our commitments.
- Brotherly love requires being prepared to mobilize our own resources.
- Brotherly love requires having compassion before we decide to help others.
- Brotherly love requires having mercy before we decide to help others.
- Brotherly love requires honoring our vows to help others.

CHAPTER 10
THE MANIFESTATION OF A MIRACLE

Have faith for the impossible

"**B**ut without faith, it is impossible to please him, for he that cometh to God must believe that he is a rewarder of them that diligently seek him" (Hebrews 11:6).

Everyone has an issue whether it is based on our grandparents' or our parents' lifestyles, blood diseases, a history of cancer, high blood pressure, cirrhosis of the liver, and/or some other life threatening disease. All of us will have to choose how we live our lives by either making a decision to ignore what is happening or take aggressive steps to deal with the dis-ease. Some of our issues require lifestyle changes that turn off the potential disease triggers to prevent the disease(s) from flaring up and/or placing us into high risk categories. If we submit ourselves to this process, God promises that He would have mercy on us and reverse the curse of these diseases.

"And God said, If thou wilt diligently hearken to the voice of the LORD thy God, and wilt do that which is right in his sight, and wilt give ear to his commandments, and keep all his statutes, I will put none of these diseases upon thee, which I have brought upon the Egyptians: for I am the LORD that healeth thee" (Exodus 15:26).

However, there are issues that we have to face that require divine intervention and we must be cognizant of the fact that divine intervention is the required currency to bring about healing and restoration in our lives. The woman with the issue of blood had suffered from her disease for years and she carried her issue after she had exhausted every possible way to be healed from what I call her "blood cancer". When we are at the weakest point in our lives, we are prime candidates for divine access, that is, the opportunity to make an appointment with the "Physician of Life". The main qualification for divine access to Him is believing that He exists and that He has the life changing powers to heal and set us free.

The Physician-Healer is here

Doctors have been trained to isolate the problem and find the best formula to stabilize the body through the applications of medicine and therapy. However, this does not discount in anyway the role of doctors in the healing process or how God works through doctors as conduits to perform healing. Nevertheless, all doctors have limitations. They sometimes can tell us what is wrong and sometimes they are baffled at what is happening because they do not know the answer to resolve the problem.

When Jesus, our Physician, started His public practice, he was deliberate and intentional regarding His purpose for what He was doing. He wanted the world to know that earthly doctors have limitations but the true Physician had come, not only to diagnose and prescribe medication, but to also provide healing and restoration to every area of our lives. That is the difference—healing us where medicine has failed. He provides hope and life to areas of our lives that we do not have access to; and He heals our diseases regardless of our condition. Jesus is a physician and a healer. No one who ever lived on the face of the earth, or in the world to come, can claim to be or perform at the level of that of a perfect physician and healer—only Jesus can. And even after He left planet earth 2000 years ago, His offices remain open 24/7, and for all eternity. **Doctors prescribe medicine, but Jesus heals us. "When Jesus heard *it*, he saith unto them, They that are whole have no need of the physician, but they that are sick: I came not to call the righteous, but sinners to repentance" (Mark 2:17).**

The Price was paid

God knew that before I was born that I would need protection from all viruses, sicknesses and diseases. This is similar to an insurance coverage plan that provides me with an escape route to live life more abundantly in the event I contract the virus of sin and/or commit any sin. This is mind blowing because there is no way humanly possible for me to afford this kind of coverage even if I were the richest man on the earth. The question is, why would God go to such extremes to provide us with such comprehensive coverage? It is true that He could just have turned a blind eye to our situation like man does and watch us self-destruct in the process. However, He decided to give us the best that He had, that is, His Son, who became the ransom or payment for our sins so that we can live. In other words, He gave His Son, who became our sacrifice or the scapegoat to buy us back and save us from the virus of sin.

The price was paid and it had to be paid by the perfect Lamb of God. No one on earth was worthy to pay it because man was infected with the virus of sin. Therefore, before we were even born in sin, the price was paid. **"But God commendeth his love toward us, in that, while we were yet sinners, Christ died for us" (Romans 5:8)**. Before we ever became sick from any dis-ease, Jesus paid the price. The price was to give not only His life but to also give us a transfusion of His blood. This gives us access to the manifestation of a miracle whenever we need it. **Without the price being paid, there is no divine intervention. Without divine intervention there is no access to the manifestation of the power of God** to restore us to our original healthy state or condition. The bottom-line is, we need God to work in our lives. We need God to show up in our lives and manifest Himself so that we can have a miracle. The price was paid so that the manifestation of our dis-ease would be totally destroyed in the flesh. **"For ye are bought with a price: therefore glorify God in your body, and in your spirit, which are God's" (1 Corinthians 6:20)**.

The Transfusion was already completed

I remember the numerous times I would be scheduled to have blood transfusions throughout my personal health challenges. I would have to sit for hours upon hours to receive blood transfusions to stabilize my blood due to low blood counts. These transfusions were administered over a period of four months and sometimes they seemed like they were an inconvenience to me because I would have to sit for more than six hours at each sitting. The point is, I needed the transfusions so I had to submit myself to the process for however long it took.

Interestingly however, many of us take for granted the process that Jesus went through for us; we are very casual and/or we seem to have little or no regard for the seriousness and commitment that He showed, and the suffering and anguish He endured, to allow us access to the manifestation of a miracle. He did not sit there like me connected to a machine for six hours drinking soft drinks and eating snacks but **"He was wounded for our transgression, bruised for our iniquities, the chastisement of our peace was upon and by his stripes we are healed" (Isaiah 53:5).** The transfusion was already completed long before we even had the capacity to get sick. The transfusion was completed long before we were born. The transfusion was completed long before the foundation of the world was created. God knew that we would need a transfusion for without it we would not, in fact, we cannot, have access to the manifestation of a miracle.

The Manifestation of a Miracle-Stem Cell Transplant

On July 25, 2013, I was admitted to hospital to undergo a stem cell transplant. Looking back in retrospect from March 20, to July 25, 2013, more than four months later, it seemed like a year had already passed given the many valleys and depths of hell that I had endured by the grace of God. I was prepared to fight for my life because, even though I had already received three rounds of intense chemotherapy, nothing was going to discourage me from seeing the hand of God manifested in my life.

During the first four days I had to undergo a final round of chemotherapy which would wipe out or compromise my immune system and prepare my body to receive new stem cells from my brother. On August 01, 2013, which is called "Day Zero", (the day new stem cells were transplanted), it was a miracle to experience how God awesomely and divinely breathe new life into my body via my bone marrow. The entire stem cell transplant process took about one hour to administer. To God be the glory!

"And the Lord shall guide thee continually, and satisfy thy soul in drought and make fat thy bones: and thou shalt be like a watered garden, and like a spring of water whose waters fail not" (Isaiah 58:11).

The days that followed were very interesting because usually when someone has a stem cell transplant, there are many complications that could potentially take place. Some include, infection, graph to host disease, reactions to medications, severe pain, vomiting, diarrhea, massive headaches, eye problems, dizziness, and loss of appetite, etc. I have also discovered that the manifestation of a miracle is never a secret, and that God's handprint is the evidence that He has performed it.

Tentatively, I was scheduled to remain in hospital under intensive care for about five weeks based on post stem cell transplant medical protocol. However, I believe with all my being that God intervened and manifested Himself in the process. How do I know and what was my confirmation of this reality? One morning, when the doctor was making his rounds, he and his team came to see me as usual. After examining me, he openly said, "Are you sure we transplant you?" This was confirmation that the Lord had manifested a miracle for me in the physical realm. My progress was significant and impressive based on blood results and his interaction with me. On August 15, 2013, (three weeks later) I was discharged from the hospital and sent home to fully recover and return for weekly clinic visits. They did not roll me out! They did not push me out! God gave me the power to rise up and walk out of that hospital room in Jesus' name. Amen!

The physical manifestation of a miracle

Whenever a miracle takes place, a physical manifestation of that miracle shows up as a confirmation of its existence. For me, there should be some outward demonstration that God had performed a miracle in my life. All of the four bone marrow biopsies were clean, indicating that there were no trace of the diagnosed condition. When I was first admitted to the hospital, I was fighting for my life and almost went into respiratory failure. Today, I do not need any artificial assistance to breathe and/or to assist my lungs in the process.

To even a greater extent, after being discharged from the hospital, following the stem cell transplant, there were no **"graph to host disease"** (**a response by the body to reject the donor cells).** Furthermore, there was no evidence of infection and my recovery, to date, is excellent. In addition, I know that I am a new creature in Christ Jesus based on the instructions given to me by my doctor. When a new born baby arrives on earth, he/she has to be taken care of differently from children who are growing and developing. I consider myself to be a new born baby with new stem cells and a new lease on life.

Here are some of the things that I should be guided by:

- No shellfish for six months;
- No raw vegetables;
- No direct skin exposure with any type of raw poultry, beef, pork, fish;
- No take-out meals;
- No dine-in at any restaurant;
- All cooked foods should be consumed within two hours of cooking;
- Do not eat cooked foods after 48 hours;
- Do not peel your own fruits;
- Limit fresh fruit to hard skins such as watermelons, cantaloupes, bananas, etc.)
- Consume at least five bottles of water a day (20 oz.)
- Eat a well balance diet;
- Get a lot of rest;

- Walk as much as possible;
- Do not interact with any type of chemicals;
- Do not participate in cleaning the house;
- Do not participate in kitchen activities;
- Avoid interactions with a lot of people directly in your presence, etc.
- Limit your sun exposure;
- Practice good hygiene to minimize infections;
- Keep your hands adequately sanitized and;
- Keep your environment sanitize as much as possible.

Even though this seems like a list from hell and may be very difficult for a normal person to follow. I realize that this has now become my new normal; and this is a small inconvenience to manage my baby status until my stem cells and immune system have been restored to acceptable levels. Praise God, the process has begun and I am anticipating its complete manifestation in my life.

Walking in the manifestation of a miracle

The manifestation of the miracle in my life means that I now have a personal commitment to God to continue walking in that manifestation. This means no more business as usual. When Jesus healed the ten leapers only one came back to say thank you after the manifestation of their miracle. To say thank you to God, I must now dedicate my life to helping and empowering people to receive the manifestation of God's awesome power, that is, I must now become a conduit for God to use me in this process. I can no longer just walk away with a gift and keep it to myself. After all, the gift is not mine to keep; but it is to be shared with those who find themselves in the place of adversity.

Timelines

The following table shows the timelines of my journey, beginning with my valley experiences to the manifestation of my miracle:

DATES (2013)	EXPERIENCES
March 16	Admitted to the local hospital Nassau
March 19	Discharged from local hospital
March 20	Air-lifted to US hospital
March 20-29, 2013	Intensive Care US hospital
March 29-Good Friday	Started 7-day Induction Chemotherapy
April 7, 2013	Completed 7-day chemotherapy
April 20, 2013	Discharged from US hospital
May 3-8, 2013	Admitted to Cancer Institute in US-Round 1 maintenance chemotherapy (five days)
June 4-10, 2013	Admitted to Cancer Institute in US-Round 2 maintenance chemotherapy (five days)
July 25, 2013	Admitted to stem cell transplant unit
July 26-29, 2013	Four days of chemotherapy in preparation for stem cell transplant
July 29-31, 2013	Two days of rest
August 01, 2013	Day zero- Transplant of donor stem cells & new birthday
August 2, 2013	Day 0 +1 - First MTX shot (*Methotrexate)
August 4, 2013	Day 0 +3 - Second MTX shot
August 7, 2013	Day 0 +6 - Third MTX shot
August 7, 2013	Day 0 + 11- Fourth MTX shot
August 15, 2013	Discharged from Cancer Institute
September 23, 2013	Removal of port from chest
September 24-present	Follow-up visits with stem cell doctor

Other Motivational Scriptures

- "When the even was come, they brought unto him many that were possessed with devils: and he cast out the spirits with *his* word, and healed all that were sick" (Matthew 8:16).

- "Jesus answered, neither hath this man sinned, nor his parents: but that the works of God should be made manifest in him" (John 9:3).
- "And he said unto her, Daughter, thy faith hath made thee whole; go in peace, and be whole of thy plague" (Mark 5:34).
- "Therefore I say unto you, what things soever ye desire, when ye pray, believe that ye receive them, and ye shall have them" (Mark 11:24).
- "Then Jesus answered and said unto her, O woman, great [is] thy faith: be it unto thee even as thou wilt. And her daughter was made whole from that very hour" (Matthew 15:28).
- "And he did not many mighty works there because of their unbelief" (Matthew 13:58).
- "Then touched he their eyes, saying, according to your faith be it done unto you" (Matthew 9:29).

Motivational Quotes

- Doctors prescribe medicine, but Jesus heals us.
- Without the price being paid, there is no divine intervention.
- Without divine intervention there is no access to the manifestation of the power of God to restore us back to our original health.
- The price was paid so that the manifestation of our dis-ease would be totally destroyed in the flesh.

CHAPTER 11
NOT EASILY SHAKEN

In God there is no unstable foundation

In late 1994, I got a call from one of my sisters who told me that my mother, who was diagnosed with cancer, had passed away. She was a strong and mighty prayer warrior. I saw the Lord use her in a great way and was a witness to many of the miracles she performed through the power of the Holy Spirit. What is also so amazing about my mother is she always found time to pray and commune with God every day. This I believe made her strong and gave her the ability to never complain about anything. Through all of her pain and suffering, she never gave up hope and fought to the finish line of life with all she had. My mother was a soldier and a warrior; she was a living example of how true Christians are supposed to live for Christ despite their current situation and disposition.

Six years later, my father also passed away from cancer. I realized later that my father was also a soldier and a warrior.

Even when he was not well he would do whatever is necessary to provide for his family regardless of how he felt or the state of his health. This too I found amazing particularly because he realized that he had an awesome responsibility to take care of his children. During many of our discussions, my father also spoke life into me. I can definitely say as one of his sons, that he was not a lazy man. In my opinion, he was a financial genius. He provided for his family, which included nine boys and four girls, with only a primary school education. I never heard my father complained or blamed anyone for where he was in life. I always saw him embraced life head-on as a quiet giant, despite being about 5'7" tall.

When I look back at both of my parents' lives and the times we shared together, I can truly say that the exemplary lives they led were big shoes to fill; their faith was not easily shaken. After all, there were some very hard times in our family. I remember the time when my father went fishing. When he came back from fishing and was bringing the boat into the dock, he had to connect the trailer to the back of the truck. My father slipped, fell and hurt his back. He became paralyzed and could not work for months. I remembered it as if it were yesterday. My mother had to do everything for him. She was a domestic engineer, and if dad did not work, no money came in for us to eat, pay bills or do things that we normally did as kids. But my mother was not easily shaken by this. Then she prayed and asked God to heal my father. Shortly afterwards, I saw my father get up out of that wheelchair and begin to walk. I was about eight or nine at the time. From that day until the day he died, my father walked like a young man. To God be the glory for parents who were not easily shaken by their valley experiences!

Don't Live in Denial

Denial is one of the most powerful weapons that the enemy uses against God's people. satan wants us to deny the fact that we are sick even though we see the manifestation of the sickness. Even though we have been diagnosed, the point is, sickness is a spirit and we should not live in denial. If we live in denial, then satan has won the battle over our sickness. **We should never deny that we have been diagnosed; but we do not have to confess and/or agree with the diagnosis.** The question is, what are we going to do? Many of us live in denial and do nothing with our diagnosis. This is called living in total ignorance. **"My people are destroyed for the lack of knowledge" (Hosea 4:6a)**.So before we start speaking in tongues, we should know what is going on in our bodies. One of my brothers, who was the donor initially, had an issue with his blood pressure. The doctor told him that his pressure medicine needs adjusting and possibly may require him taking another medication to better manage his blood pressure.

We went for follow-up visits to another doctor that same day and he re-checked his pressure. My brother and I were not in denial regarding his blood pressure; and we agreed to pray that the spirit of high blood pressure would leave his body so that he would be cleared to donate his stem cells to me. So we prayed, and I was deliberate and direct with my prayer: "I come against this spirit of high blood pressure; I command it to leave my brother and let him go." Miraculously, his blood pressure normalized. On Thursday, two days later, my brother had a follow-up meeting with the doctor. They checked his blood pressure and cleared him to contribute his stem cells to me for the transplant. **"God is an awesome God!**

Can you imagine if I had panicked and started applying pressure to my brother by blaming him for his pressure being high? However, I was not easily shaken! I knew that my brother was destined by God to give me his stem cells before the foundation of the world. In the physical, it appeared that the process would be stopped, because without my brother's clearance, I would not be able to use his cells to get a stem cell transplant.

Understand what is happening

Many of us are clueless about what is going on when we are diagnosed with sickness. We do not want to associate ourselves with the stigma of the big "C" word. We do not do any research on our diagnosed condition, and we do not seek counsel from those who are experts in the field. I remember when I was diagnosed with acute myeloid leukemia, circumstances prevented me from doing any research on acute myeloid leukemia. I remembered having meetings with the hospital pharmacist, the stem cell coordinator, the stem cell transplant doctor, the cardiologist, and the pulmonary specialist. I had an echocardiogram, EKGs, stress tests, chest x-rays, extensive blood works, and my profile developed, etc. Based on all of these tests, I made sure that all of the professionals who were involved in managing my care explained in lay-men terms the finer details of what was going on in my body. Surprisingly, I listened attentively, took notes, and asked questions, although I forgot to ask certain questions. However, when I saw some of them again, I made sure all of my questions and queries were answered. This is the ultimate goal—to be informed.

Once informed, I could go to God with a shopping list of items that I needed to pray for, and ultimately get deliverance.

I needed to be deliberate because the diagnosed condition required me to become deliberate and specific in my approach to God. In addition, when I prayed and cast out demon spirits, I was well informed and knowledgeable about which demon spirit I was casting out. This gave me the power I needed so that I was not easily shaken. I knew who I was going up against, and because I had the right information, I was able to isolate each demon that was trying to rise up against me in judgment and cast him out.

Some of us do not want to go to the doctor. We take home remedies to try and solve the problem ourselves. Whether we realize it or not we are deceiving ourselves and the truth is not in us. Why are we trying to diagnose a medical problem and we do not have medical training and/or the expertise? Some of us are closet doctors, we know everything that should be done because we experience some of the same symptoms that our friends and/or loved ones have experienced. However, they do not have the level of expertise to experiment on us. What should we do? Go to the doctor and let him/her diagnose the problem. This does not limit God. As a matter of fact, when you go to God, you can give him the doctor's report and leave it at the cross for Jesus to deal with. It is no longer your problem but God's problem, the Healer of all problems.

No more Secrets

There was a man who spent most of his life working hard to take care of his family. He placed his personal agenda regarding what he wanted to do in life on hold. As the man began to age, he did not take care of himself in the manner that he should. Every year he knew that he should take a PSA test (a test that looks for cancer in the prostate). He failed to take this test or go to the doctor for his annual exam due to his fear and cultural stereotyping. Six months later, he started experiencing problems with his sexual organs. He suffered from urinary blockage, slow stream and an inability to maintain an erection. Continuing to live in fear, he decided not to go to the hospital and, thus, kept his undiagnosed condition a secret. A few years later, the doctor confirmed that he had prostate cancer; and it was in its advanced stage and he later passed away.

Sickness is a dis-ease so we have every right to petition our God to deliver us from that demonic spirit. satan goes literally head over heels when he discovers that we are refusing to seek medical help, find someone we can talk to, and/or get help on the best way forward.

Many of us would keep sickness a secret, and then the secret would begin to have a negative impact on our walk with God and their relationship with their family members. God does not want us to hide the entrapment strategies of the devil; he wants us to expose him for what he has done. **"And having spoiled principalities and powers; he made a shew of them, openly, triumphing over them in it" (Colossians 2:15).** We need to serve notice on the devil and stop allowing him to control us by keeping secrets regarding our health condition. This is no time to become a wimp; there is no need to be afraid and/or fearful of the consequences of the dis-ease. The Lord is our Redeemer and our strength. He will heal and deliver us from the snares of the enemy.

Call for Back-up!

When a house catches fire, neighbors call the fire department. When a man has been shot, someone calls 911 or the police department. Old school friends that we have not seen in twenty (20) years and persons who have participated in get-rich quick schemes are usually at the top of our call list when we need someone to financially bail us out of a desperate situation. God is not like a man, who, when we need him, goes on vacation, or promises to come to our rescue but never shows up and gives no explanation concerning why he did not show up. God is our back-up for He always comes to our rescue, and never lets us down. **"God is our refuge and strength, a very present help in trouble" (Psalm 46:1).**

When are we going to start calling in for our back-up to the Source that has the power and the capacity to deliver us when we call? Why do we call on our back-up after satan has totally annihilate us? We give satan too much credit and promotion for work that he has not done. The best thing we can do for ourselves is call for back-up when satan comes after us. Call for back-up to the True and Living God.

> **"And he said, Harken ye, all Judah, and ye inhabitants of Jerusalem, and thou King Jehoshaphat. Thus saith the Lord unto you, be not afraid nor dismayed by reason of this multitude; for the battle is not yours but God's" (2 Chronicles 20:15).**

Live in the Now

Remember when some of us bought our first car? We were excited when we drove it off the lot. We went to the extent of washing that car almost every day after work to keep it clean. If we had a girlfriend, we were very excited to take her for the first ride. Five years later, the same car is banged up, the wheels wobble, and the car runs hot and refuses to budge, leaving us stranded on the side of the road. When we think about it we have good memories of that new car; but that was in the past. Now, we are living in the now and have some decisions to make. We can either get a new car (healing) in the now or we can spend the rest of our lives thinking about the past (the diagnosed condition), by focusing on the memory, or by erecting a monument, of something we chose not to change. There is no healing in the past. We have to forgive and let it go. If we do not forgive, it will cripple our ability to enjoy living in the now where there is healing and restoration. The now is all we have as a starting point to aim for the future.

When we think about it, **our now's help us to mold and shape our tomorrows**. But some of us are so obsessed with our future that we schedule out of our daily routine the time to enjoy life now. We have to enjoy the now. I remember, before I was diagnosed, I was always on the run, trying to catch the future. I had very little time to enjoy the finer things of life. It was not until I was in the hospital, with nowhere to go, that I realized that I needed to live in the now. All of the appointments I had, the meetings that I had scheduled, the amount of workload that remained outstanding, all became inconsequential. It is amazing, if we take the time to stop and think about it, how much of life we can truly enjoy without all of the stress that life presents if we just live in the now.

Have Relentless Faith

Some people may think that I am crazy for writing this book during the time I was going through the process of being totally and completely healed. I share a different opinion, one that is grounded in the Word of God and my character that began to form from the day I was born, 47 years ago during Hurricane Betsy in 1965. I believe that if we are going into a fight we must be prepared and ready to totally annihilate the enemy. There is no time 'to play panny-cake' and sing nursery rhymes. The reasons for being normal is over; the time has come to be radical and relentless in our faith in God.

We may think that one morning we can wake up and have relentless faith. **Relentless faith does not come in an overnight package or prepared in a microwave.** Relentless faith comes as we walk it out, fight for it and build it up every day of our lives; it comes through our friendships, our experiences, God's Word, and our commitment to the Lord Jesus Christ. This book is a testament of my relentless faith and trust in God, and it plays an active role in my healing process. With it, I am doing whatever is necessary, and whatever is at my disposal, to collaborate with God so that I can receive my total and complete healing. I will not argue because there were many tough, hell wrenching, dark and cloudy days. Nevertheless, I pressed my way through, I pushed myself, and I cried out to God so that His goodness and mercy would follow me. I prayed in my darkest hours and found peace; and I held God accountable for His Word. Prayerfully, I believed God, and was convinced that I was not **Easily Shaken**. I was not **Easily Shaken**, not by my strength, or by my power, but by standing on the Solid Rock, which is Jesus Christ our Lord!

The Ten-second Rule

All of us at some time or the other will have to go into the boxing ring of life, whether we think we have been forced to or we have been challenged to defend what we believe. **"These things I have spoken unto you, that in me ye might have peace. In the world ye shall have tribulation: but be of good cheer; I have overcome the world" (John 16:33).** No one is exempt from the boxing ring of life because it has been destined for us. It is like a road we all have to travel. Some boxing rings of life are teaser rounds or matches that we fight and come out with minor scratches and bruises. The end result is, we won the match. Then there are times when we enter the ring of life unaware of its intensity, and the blow we receive in the first few seconds of the match hits us flat on our faces. We should not be caught by surprise because at some point in our lives we should expect to be time-tested.

When two boxers, who are opponents, go into the ring, two goals are ultimately clear. One, each enter the ring with the mentality that both are champions, who are going to win the boxing match. Two, they also enter the ring with the mentality that, since they have prepared or trained for the fight, they will do everything within their power to force their opponent to comply with the ten-second rule. As the fight begins, some punches are harder than others, some are missed and, as time goes by, both boxers seek to win the fight by scoring the most points, and/or by delivering a TKO (technical knock- out). There is nothing wrong with us when life hits us down now and again. There is nothing wrong with us when we have to overcome challenges that seek to drive us out of our minds and leave us decrepit. We are normal and should expect them.

However, we should not allow ourselves to go down as defeated contenders. We have ten-seconds to make up our minds about what we are going to do. Ten seconds is a long-time to think about a strategy whether or not we should fight or surrender in defeat. Ten seconds is a long-time to consider how we should respond to our crisis or life's unexpected turns and challenges. The only way to overcome these challenges, and not be easily shaken, is to get up in nine seconds, even if getting up is the only strategy available to you so that you can stay in the ring of life. This is a sign that you have the confidence, faith, tenacity and willpower to overcome in the face of adversity. This lets your opponent know that in the midst of it all, standing your ground is the only option of survival for you until your change comes.

I wish to encourage you to take a stand and face life's up and downs with the courage and confidence that God gives us the power and ability to be more than conquerors in Christ Jesus our Lord. **"Nay, in all these things we are more than conquerors through him that loved us" (Romans 8:3)**. Refuse to be **Easily Shaken** whenever you have to face life's adversities, for God is more than able to deliver us. Amen and Amen!

I believe without a shadow of a doubt that God has totally and completely healed me from the crown of my head to the soul of my feet; and from March 16, 2013 when this journey began to October 8, 2013, I have seen God delivered me in a mighty way. I have also seen the manifestation of God's healing in my life everyday as I continue weekly follow-up with my doctor. My doctor has advised me that at the end of December 2013, I will be going back home to the Bahamas based on my current progress. To God be the glory; and mighty are the handiworks of the Lord of Creation.

Other Motivational Scriptures

- "Therefore, my beloved brethren, be ye steadfast, unmovable, always abounding in the work of the Lord, forasmuch as ye know that your labor is not in vain in the Lord" (I Corinthians 15:58).
- "Stand fast therefore in the liberty wherewith Christ hath made us free, and be not entangled again with the yoke of bondage" (Galatians 5:1).
- "A man shall not be established by wickedness: but the root of the righteous shall not be moved" (Proverbs 12:3).
- "For the king trusteth in the LORD, and through the mercy of the most High he shall not be moved" (Psalm 21:7).

Motivational Quotes

- Denial is one of the most powerful weapons that the enemy uses against God's people.
- Never deny that you have been diagnosed.
- Do not confess and/or agree with the diagnosis.

Finally, Lord I submit this book to you as my living testament of your goodness; so that you will get the glory in Jesus name, Thank you for the opportunity to be a conduit that your name will be glorified throughout the earth. Thank you for good success. Amen!